CHRISTMAS IS COMING
A resource book for teachers

Redvers Brandling

Basil Blackwell

Acknowledgements

My thanks are, as ever, due to the staff and children of Dewhurst St Mary School, from whom I constantly learn so much! I also received a great deal of help from Kwet Lunts, Sue Payne, 'Freddy', Sally Furness, Peter Stephens, Anne Mottershead, Cliff Dix, Brian Miller, Peter Westmore, Robin Osborne, Dennis Patten and Vic Winfield.

The author and publisher would like to thank the following for giving permission to reproduce copyright material:

André Deutsch: 'Christmas Dinner' by Michael Rosen, from *Quick, Let's Get Out of Here,* Michael Rosen and Quentin Blake;
Central Board of Finance of the Church of England: 'Hymn for St Nicholas' by Jennie Bowen; and 'Sam and the Midnight Music' by Pamela Egan, from *Together* Magazine, Nov/Dec 1982;
Collins: 'Coming Home', from *Swings and Roundabouts,* Mick Gowar;
David Higham Associates Ltd: 'A Child's Christmas', from *A Child's Christmas,* Dylan Thomas (published by Dent);
Mowbrays: 'What Really Happened?', from *The First Christmas – what really happened?,* H. J. Richards;
Penguin Books Ltd: 'Only Show', from *Please Mrs Butler,* Allan Ahlberg (published by Kestrel Books).

© 1985 Redvers Brandling
First published 1985
Reprinted 1986, 1987

Published by
Basil Blackwell Limited
108 Cowley Road
Oxford OX4 1JF
England

British Library Cataloguing in Publication Data

Brandling, Redvers
 Christmas is coming: A resource book for teachers.
 1. Christmas   2. Education of children
 I. Title
 372.19   BV1475.2
 ISBN 0 631 14147 2

Typeset in 10 on 12pt Times Roman
by Katerprint Co. Ltd, Oxford
Printed in Great Britain

Contents

Introduction

I have found, in many years of teaching, that teachers in infant, junior, middle and lower secondary schools approach their Christmas preparations with a rare combination of enthusiasm, anticipation, resourcefulness – and durability! All recognise the need for long-term planning and detailed preparation as prerequisites for the myriad of activities which take place in school at this time of the year. This book seeks to provide some help with such planning.

The book's structure derives from the intention to provide twelve paths along which work related to Christmas might be pursued. Within these paths are poetry, plays, facts, anecdotes, interviews, opinions, reflections, descriptions and practical suggestions.

R.B.
1985

Reference books

Who is Father Reference? by Shirley Harrison (David and Charles), is a most useful reference and the source for 'A parcel for Christmas'. A variation of the 'Number Fun' idea first appeared in *A Book of Practical Ideas for the Primary School*, Redvers Brandling (Ward Lock Educational). Neither 'Christmas Day' nor 'Long Long Ago' have a known author but the source for both was *Seeing and Doing* (Thames Television, 1977). The story 'One Good Turn Deserves Another' was adapted from the book *Japanese Children's Favourite Stories*, presented to Dewhurst St Mary School by Mr T. Morishita of Nishi, Miki City, Japan. The details of how Terry Biddlecomb spent Christmas come from *Winner's Disclosure* (Stanley Paul). The idea for the Christmas 'Who dunnit?' came from a story in *The Magnet Detective Book*, Wolfgang Ecke (Magnet).

Chapter 1

Christmas readings

The purpose of this chapter is to provide a series of readings which tell the Christmas story very simply. The aim has been to keep the passages easy to read. It is hoped that these readings might be useful in initiating classroom work and discussion; as perhaps a series of introductions to assemblies leading up to Christmas; as part of a service involving the traditional nine lessons.

Each of the readings is followed by a Biblical reference so that source material can be consulted, and the chapter ends with some additional background information for the teacher.

The Christmas story

Reading 1   Joseph and Mary

Nearly two thousand years ago two people, called Joseph and Mary, lived in a small town called Nazareth. They were very happy because they were to be married.

One night a strange and wonderful thing happened to Mary. She saw an angel who told her that she was going to have a baby boy. The angel went on to tell her that this would be a very special baby indeed.

'You will call him Jesus,' said the angel, 'and he will be a King who reigns for ever.'

Joseph and Mary felt honoured and they began to make preparations for the coming of the baby. Joseph, who was a carpenter, made a cradle, and there was a great feeling of excitement as the time for the baby to be born came nearer.

Then Joseph received some very worrying news.

(Ref: Luke 1, vs. 26–36)

Reading 2   Caesar Augustus

At the time Mary was about to have her baby, the land in which she and Joseph lived was ruled by the Romans. The Roman Emperor was called Caesar Augustus.

Caesar Augustus wanted to be sure that he knew how many people lived in the lands the Romans ruled. This was so that he could make all the people pay taxes.

'The best way to find this out,' said Caesar Augustus, 'is to make every man go back to the town where he was born, and then sign a register there.'

Orders were sent out to tell everybody to do this. When Joseph heard the news he hurried to tell Mary.

'I'm afraid it's bad news,' he said. 'I've got to go to Bethlehem, and because you are my wife you must come too.'

'But the baby, Joseph,' replied Mary. 'It will take us days to get there . . .'

'And you can be sure it will be very crowded when we do arrive,' said Joseph. Then he explained to Mary why they had no choice. They must go to Bethlehem. Mary began to prepare for the journey.

(Ref: Luke 2, vs. 1–6)

Reading 3   The journey

Joseph and Mary set off from Nazareth to Bethlehem. Joseph went in front, leading a donkey, on which Mary rode.

It was a very difficult journey. During the days they had to climb up high, rough ground and at night it was bitterly cold. As Joseph covered his sleeping wife with his thick coat made of sheep's wool, he worried about getting her safely to Bethlehem.

As the journey went on Mary and Joseph met more and more people going in the same direction. All the men had been born in Bethlehem and they were taking their families back there with them to be registered by the Romans.

'It's going to be crowded there,' said one of the men to Joseph.

'Yes, I know,' replied Joseph, 'and I must find somewhere comfortable for my wife.'

Joseph got more and more worried, but Mary never complained. She was sure that everything would be all right.

Then, late one afternoon, they saw Bethlehem ahead of them. It stood, high on a hillside, and the smoke from hundreds of fires drifted upwards. These had been lit by people who were camping outside the city. It was freezing cold.

(Ref: Luke 2, vs. 3–5)

Reading 4   No room at the inn

When Joseph and Mary passed through the gates and into the city of Bethlehem it was almost dark. The streets were packed.

Men, women, children, young and old, pushed and jostled each other. There were loud cries from traders who were trying to sell everything from sweets to goats. Some people looked as if they were enjoying the excitement, others looked lost and miserable.

'Excuse me,' said Joseph, stopping a man, 'can you tell me where I can find an inn? I must get a room for my wife.'

'Not a chance,' said the man roughly, 'everywhere is full. You won't get a room tonight.'

Joseph went on. By now Mary looked very tired and even the donkey looked as if it could go no further. For almost two more hours Joseph searched. He could find nowhere, and then, when he had reached the far edge of the town he saw a small inn. It was his last hope. Passing the lighted windows he knocked at the heavy wooden door. A voice called out from inside.

'Go away whoever you are. We're full up. There is no room at this inn.'

Joseph paused, if only he could talk to the landlord and explain. He knocked again but nothing happened. He knocked again, much harder.

Suddenly the door was flung open and a large man stood in the door way. He was obviously angry.

'Didn't you hear what I said? There's no room in this inn, now go . . .'

He stopped speaking. He had seen beyond Joseph, to the pale, cold and weary Mary.

'I wouldn't ask for myself,' said Joseph, 'but my wife is going to have a baby. I must find somewhere for her.'

'Well,' said the landlord. 'I really have no rooms left, but if you just walk to the end of this building you will find a stable. You're welcome to spend the night there.'

(Ref: Luke 2, vs. 6–7)

Reading 5   The birth

When the landlord told Mary and Joseph they could stay in the stable they were overjoyed. The stable was just like a small cave but there was a pile of clean straw in the corner.

'Look,' said Joseph, 'this will make a perfect cradle.'

Taking some of the clean straw, he carried it to a manger which the animals used to eat from. Emptying the manger, Joseph then filled it with clean straw.

Meanwhile Mary was making her preparations for the birth of Jesus. New babies were wrapped in swaddling clothes to keep them warm. Mary laid out her swadddling clothes, and soon afterwards the baby Jesus was born. (Ref: Luke 2, v. 7)

Reading 6   In the fields

While Joseph and Mary were making preparations for the birth of the baby some shepherds in the fields outside the town were settling down for the night. They were gathered round a fire on a dark hillside. The light thrown off by the flames helped them to watch their sheep and see that none escaped. The shepherds' dogs lay sleeping beside the fire.

Suddenly, and completely unexpectedly, the sky was filled with a brilliant light. The shepherds were terrified and covered their faces as they crouched nearer to the ground. Then the voice of an angel spoke to them.

'Do not be afraid, for behold, I bring you good news of great joy which will come to all people.'

Cautiously the shepherds lifted their heads, and the angel went on to tell them of the baby which had just been born in Bethlehem . . . 'a baby wrapped in swaddling clothes and lying in a manger.'

Then there were the voices of more than one angel. It sounded as if there were hundreds, and they were all singing:

> 'Glory to God in the highest,
> And peace to all people on earth.'

Then, as if nothing had ever happened, it was dark and silent again. The shepherds stayed still, hardly daring to move. Then one of them stood up.

'We must do something,' he said. 'We must go to Bethlehem at once and find this baby.'

At this they all started to talk at once. They felt a great sense of excitement. Leaving the dogs to guard the flocks of sheep they set off for the town. (Ref: Luke 2, vs. 8–14)

Reading 7   The shepherds

By the time the shepherds reached Bethlehem the first signs of dawn were lighting up the sky. Hurrying through the empty streets they passed the inn and came to the door of the stable. A light shone from underneath it. The leading shepherd knocked on the door.

Almost immediately it was opened by Joseph. He beckoned to the shepherds to come in. Moving quietly, the shepherds crowded into the stable. Jesus awoke as they did so.

'It is exactly as the angel told us,' said one of the shepherds, and they knelt down beside the manger. They told Joseph and Mary what had happened in the fields, and then gave their presents of a lamb for the child, and milk and wool for Mary and Joseph.

'I am sorry the presents are not fit for a king,' said the leading shepherd, 'but we are very poor people.'

'I think,' replied Joseph, 'that you were the first people chosen to see Jesus because you are poor.'

The shepherds then left the stable and went out into the town. By now it was morning and the streets were filling with people. The shepherds told everyone they met about the marvellous happenings of the night.
(Ref: Luke 2, vs. 8–18)

Reading 8   The star

At the same time as the angels were appearing to the shepherds in the fields, a strange thing was happening in another part of the world.

A new and brilliant star suddenly appeared in the sky. Three wise men, who lived in the East, saw the star. Each knew immediately that they must follow this star because it would lead them to where a new king was born.

The three wise men were called Caspar, Melchior and Balthazar. When they set off on their journey they took with them valuable presents to give to the new king. One of the presents was gold; another was frankincense which is used to make air smell sweet; and the third was myrrh, an ointment.

Unlike Mary, the three wise men did not travel on donkeys. They had fine camels, with plenty of servants to look after them. But the journey they had to make was a very long one and they followed the star for many days. Eventually it stopped over Bethlehem.
(Ref: Matthew 2, vs. 10–12)

Reading 9   The wise men

By the time the three wise men, who were also known as kings, had arrived in Bethlehem, Mary and Joseph had moved out of the stable into a small house.

After the shepherds had told everybody the news the baby had many visitors – but none so splendid as the three kings.

'Just look at those magnificent clothes,' gasped a woman as the kings passed by.

'And those camels,' said a man.

'And all those servants,' said another.

They must be very important people,' said the first man, as he watched the wise men go to the room where Mary and Joseph were now staying with Jesus.

After the kings, and as many people as possible, had crowded into the room, a strange thing happened. When the kings saw Jesus they immediately knelt down, just as the humble shepherds had done. Then they presented their gifts.

Everybody watching realised that this was another very special occasion. Truly this was a great king who had been born.
(Ref: Matthew 2, vs. 10–12)

Background information

Whilst these passages and references could be used directly, it might be useful to have some further background information for use in discussion. The following is therefore intended to be supplementary material which might help in this context.

Palestine had become part of the Roman Empire in the year 65 BC. Prior to this it had suffered at the hands of Assyria, Babylon, Persia and Greece, and the great triumphs of David's reign were looked back upon with longing. The excitement at the birth of a 'new King' was therefore intense – although ultimately the enormous influence of Jesus was not quite in the way these patriots expected.

The readings given in this chapter deal in a very simple manner with the 'three wise men' and ignore Herod completely. However, the stories of both are interwoven and significant.

Herod, King of Judea, was born an Arab but had established himself with the Romans. Naturally he wanted this situation to continue, and he had both the power and temperament to try and make sure that it did, no matter how ruthless the necessary measures. Like everyone else he soon heard of the birth of the 'new King' in Bethlehem and he enlisted the help of the three wise men to find this threat to his authority. He asked them to tell him where Jesus was when they found him (Matthew 2, vs. 7–8). Initially under the impression that Herod too wanted to come and worship, the wise men had a dream which foretold of his real intent. As a result they made their way back to the East without giving Herod the information he sought.

Frustrated and furious Herod instigated the killing of all boys under two years in Bethlehem. Mary and Joseph had also had a dream warning them of the danger, and they left the city in time. The slaughter of the children left behind is commemorated on Holy Innocents' Day, 28 December.

There is much in the story of the three kings which is symbolic. As they were supposedly white, black and yellow skinned they symbolised all the world's races; and their gifts, gold symbolising kingship, frankincense – holiness, and myrrh – suffering and death, portrayed key features in the life of Jesus.

Chapter 2

Words for Christmas

This chapter is pot pourri of stories – true and fictional, and poems. Some relate to Christmas past, others concern events of today, and there is one specially-written 'ghost story with special effects' for a dark winter afternoon.

'Dear Santa Claus . . .'

Louise switched on her television set and settled down to watch the Johnny Carson show. Soon she was watching, and listening to, Johnny Carson reading out some letters which children had written to Santa Claus.

As she watched she began to think . . . who read the letters children wrote to Santa Claus in the town where she lived, did anybody, were any of them ever answered? Louise lived in the town of San Antonio, Texas, a very big city in the United States of America. She went to see the Chief Post Master to find out.

The answer she got was that the letters were not even opened. Determined to do something about this Louise persuaded the Post Master to open the letters, and pass them on to her. When she read them through, thirteen seemed to be from deserving children who did not appear to have very much. Louise then had another idea – why couldn't she act as Santa Claus?

Calling on all her friends she explained the situation, and soon had thirteen presents. These she left on the doorsteps of the thirteen letter writers, and nobody knew how they had got there, except for 'Santa Claus!'

The next Christmas Louise began to prepare a little earlier. Calling on shops, stores and businesses she asked for anything that would help – money, damaged toys, time, skills. When the letters started to come in she was prepared, and even managed to produce a Christmas tree for a little girl who had written to say her family was too poor to ever have one.

By now the newspapers had heard about Louise and stories about her work began to get printed. As a result more people got to know about what she was doing, and offered to help. This was just as well because after answering those thirteen letters in her first year, Louise found that each year the number grew – 250 . . . 1000 . . . finally up to 20 000.

By now Louise could not possible do all the work herself, but help came from all sides. She was loaned a huge building called Fort Sam Houston in which to work; money was given from many businesses and people in San Antonio, and all kinds of helpers came forward. Meeting in Fort Sam Houston they repaired toys, arranged for them to go to the correct letter writers, wrapped parcels, answered telephone calls – and two hundred of them became 'Santa Clauses' who delivered the presents.

Louise's idea has not only been a wonderful one for the children of San Antonio, it has also been something marvellous for the helpers. They include senior citizens, people who have been ill, and others who have been in trouble with the police. Getting together to do something for other people has been an unforgettable experience for all of them.

Only Snow

Outside, the sky was almost brown.
The clouds were hanging low.
Then all of a sudden it happened:
The air was full of snow.

The children rushed to the windows.
The teacher let them go,
Though she teased them for their foolishness.
After all, it was only snow.

It was only snow that was falling,
Only out of the sky,
Only on to the turning earth
Before the blink of an eye.

What else could it do from up there,
But fall in the usual way?
It was only weather, really.
What else could you say?

The teacher sat at her desk
Putting ticks in a little row,
While the children stared through steamy glass
At the only snow.

Allan Ahlberg

The Christmas fire

It was on the afternoon of the day of Christmas Eve, and I was in Mrs Prothero's garden, waiting for cats, with her son Jim. It was snowing. It was always snowing at Christmas. December, in my memory, is white as Lapland, though there were no reindeers. But there were cats. Patient, cold and callous, our hands wrapped in socks, we waited to snowball the cats. Sleek and long as jaguars and horrible-whiskered, spitting and snarling, they would slink and sidle over white back-garden walls, and the lynx-eyed hunters, Jim and I, fur-capped and moccasined trappers from Hudson Bay, off Mumbles Road, would hurl our deadly snowballs at the green of their eyes.

The wise cats never appeared. We were so still, Eskimo-footed arctic marksmen in the muffling silence of the eternal snows – eternal since Wednesday – that we never heard Mrs Prothero's first cry from her igloo at the bottom of the garden. Or, if we heard it at all, it was, to us, like the far-off challenge of our enemy and prey, the neighbour's polar cat. But soon the voice grew louder. 'Fire!' cried Mrs Prothero, and she beat the dinner-gong.

And we ran down the garden, with the snowballs in our arms, toward the house; and smoke, indeed, was pouring out of the dining-room, and the gong was bombilating, and Mrs Prothero was announcing ruin like a town crier in Pompeii. This was better than all the cats in Wales standing on the wall in a row. We bounded into the house, laden with snowballs, and stopped at the open door of the smoke-filled room.

Something was burning all right; perhaps it was Mr Prothero, who always slept there after midday dinner with a newspaper over his face. But he was standing in the middle of the room, saying, 'A fine Christmas!' and smacking at the smoke with a slipper. 'Call the fire brigade,' cried Mrs Prothero as she beat the gong.

'They won't be there,' said Mr Prothero, 'it's Christmas.'

There was no fire to be seen, only clouds of smoke and Mr Prothero standing in the middle of them, waving his slippers as though he was conducting.

'Do something,' he said.

And we threw all our snowballs into the smoke – I think we missed Mr Prothero – and ran out of the house to the telephone box.

'Let's call the police as well,' Jim said.

'And the ambulance,'

'And Ernie Jenkins, he likes fires.'

But we only called the fire brigade, and soon the fire engine came and three tall men in helmets brought a hose into the house and Mr Prothero got out just in time before they turned it on. Nobody could have had a noisier Christmas Eve. And when the firemen turned off the hose and were standing

in the wet, smoky room, Jim's aunt, Miss Prothero, came downstairs and peered in at them. Jim and I waited, very quietly, to hear what she would say to them. She said the right thing, always. She looked at the three tall firemen in their shining helmets, standing among the smoke and cinders and dissolving snowballs, and she said: 'Would you like something to read?'
From *A Child's Christmas in Wales*, Dylan Thomas

Chrisimas Day

There was a pig went out to dig,
Chrisimas day, Chrisimas day,
There was a pig went out to dig
On Chrisimas day in the morning.

There was a cow went out to plough,
Chrisimas day, Chrisimas day,
There was a cow went out to plough
On Chrisimas day in the morning.

There was a sparrow went out to harrow,
Chrisimas day, Chrisimas day,
There was a sparrow went out to harrow
On Chrisimas day in the morning.

There was a drake went out to rake,
Chrisimas day, Chrisimas day,
There was a drake went out to rake
On Chrisimas day in the morning.

There was a crow went out to sow,
Chrisimas day, Chrisimas day,
There was a crow went out to sow
On Chrisimas day in the morning.

There was a sheep went out to reap,
Chrisimas day, Chrisimas day,
There was a sheep went out to reap
On Chrisimas day in the morning.

(Author unknown)

Ivor's Christmas gift

Ivor was a carpenter. One Christmas he wanted to carve the best piece of work he had ever done. He had heard that a prince had been born at the castle. He hoped to give his carving to the prince as a gift.

'First of all the wood, then the tools . . . then, the horse,' thought Ivor to himself. What he intended to make for the prince was a magnificent wooden rocking horse. Two weeks before Christmas he started.

Slowly a beautiful horse began to take shape. Ivor was so engrossed in his work that he forgot to eat, and almost forgot to sleep. He sang as he worked.

One day a poor young orphan boy came begging at Ivor's door. He knocked three times but Ivor didn't hear him – he was too busy working on the horse. The boy pushed open the door and went inside. He gasped.

'Cor . . .'

'What . . . what is it?' asked Ivor. 'Who are you, how did you get in?'

'It's great.'

'What?'

'I've never seen anything like it. It's great.'

Ivor smiled, put down his chisel, and looked at the pale, thin, ragged boy.

'Thank you,' he said. 'It's a rocking horse I'm making for the new prince. Now what can I do for you?'

For a moment the boy hesitated. All thoughts of food, money, time to get warmed – the things he usually asked for – fled from his mind as he looked at the wonderful, carved wooden horse.

'Will you . . .?' he stopped.

'Will I what?' asked Ivor.

'Will you . . . make me something?' whispered the boy.

'Here,' said Ivor, 'sit down here by the fire.'

When the boy had done so Ivor gave him a hot drink and something to eat, and then picked up his tools and a small piece of wood.

The boy watched, fascinated, as the craftsman's hands moved with skill and care. In what seemed like only a few minutes a tiny carved horse lay in Ivor's hands

'There,' smiled Ivor, 'take this little horse for yourself and I hope it brings you luck.'

The boy stammered his thanks and with the little horse clasped tightly in his hands he shuffled back outside into the cold. Ivor immediately went back to work on the rocking horse.

The days quickly went by, until it was Christmas Eve.

'Now to deliver my present to the prince,' thought Ivor. He looked at the result of all his hours and hours of work. It stood there like a real and magnificent horse. Carved exquisitely and painted in beautiful shades, it rocked at the touch of a finger. Carefully Ivor loaded it onto his cart and wrapped it in blankets to protect it. Then he set off for the palace.

After half a day's walk, dragging the heavy cart over the snowy forest tracks Ivor arrived at the palace. He crossed the drawbridge and rang the bell outside the massive gate. A metal grille shot back in the gate and a harsh face peered out.

'What do you want?'

'Oh . . . I've come to bring a present for the new prince.'

'Why should the prince want anything from you? Be off with you!'

'But it's a special present, I've spent . . .'

'Don't stand there arguing,' snarled the guard. 'Clear off or else I'll come out there and help you on your way.'

As the guard finished speaking there was the sudden clatter of horses' hooves and a haughty voice shouted, 'Get that gate open!'

'At once,' replied the guard, in a very different tone of voice, and the great gate began to rise slowly upwards.

Ivor saw a coach and horses waiting on the other side. He could see into the coach and there, cradled in his mother's arms was the prince! Now he would be able to deliver his present.

The gate clanked as it reached its full height, and Ivor stepped into the middle of the drawbridge.

'Your majesty . . .' he began.

But the coach drove straight at him. Its occupants stared straight ahead as if he wasn't there and the coachman lashed out savagely at him with his whip.

'But . . .' cried Ivor, then a blow from the whip sent him reeling back into the snow-covered banks of the moat. His cart was swept aside by the rushing coach and both it, and the beautiful carved rocking horse, finished up in the ditch with him.

'But why?' Ivor muttered to himself as he wiped the snow from his face. 'I only wanted to give them something.' It was then that he noticed he was not alone in the ditch.

Another body lay there almost covered by snow. It was tiny, ragged – and in its hand it clutched a small, wooden horse.

Forgetting his bleeding face Ivor scrambled through the snow and tenderly brushed the wet hair from the tiny face. For a moment he thought the boy was dead, and then he saw a barely noticeable movement of the chest. Without wasting a second Ivor rushed to where his cart lay on its side. Dragging it upright he gasped with relief when he saw that its wheels were unbroken. Hurriedly he threw the rocking horse on one side of the cart and scrambled back to where the boy lay. Cradling the tiny figure in his arms Ivor laid him gently on the cart and wrapped the blankets he had used to cover the horse tightly round him. Having done this he set off back to his cottage as quickly as he could.

It was dark when the exhausted carpenter reached the cottage. The little boy still had not stirred. Once inside Ivor ignored his own tiredness and got to work. First he put the boy in his large comfortable bed and then set to work to build a fire as quickly as he could. When the fire was blazing he boiled a large tin bath of water and then carried it to the bed.

Taking off the boy's tattered clothes Ivor washed him with the hot water and then wrapped him warmly in some old thick shirts he had. The boy now seemed to be breathing more normally and a little colour had crept into his cheeks.

By now it was dawn and Ivor went outside again to the cart, took down the carved rocking horse and carried it into the cottage.

He put it at the foot of the bed and began to make a drink to give to the boy when he awoke.

For a second or two he must have dozed because he was suddenly awakened by the sound of bells ringing.

'It's Christmas!' he said to himself, and gave a slow smile.

Then, when he turned, he saw that the boy's eyes were open.

'Am I in heaven?' asked a small voice.

'Why do you ask?' said Ivor.

'Because I can't remember when I was so warm before,' said the boy, 'and I've still got my horse.' He held up a frail hand, clutching the tiny horse Ivor had made him.

Ivor smiled. 'You're not in heaven – but you've come home, and,' he nodded to the foot of the bed, 'you've got two horses.'

Winter Time

Late lies the wintry sun a-bed,
A frosty, fiery sleepy-head;
Blinks but an hour or two; and then,
A blood-red orange, sets again.

Before the stars have left the skies,
At morning in the dark I rise;
And shivering in my nakedness,
By the cold candle, bathe and dress.

Close by the jolly fire I sit
To warm my frozen bones a bit;
Or, with reindeer-sled, explore
The colder countries round the door.

When to go out, my nurse doth wrap
Me in my comforter and cap;
The cold wind burns my face, and blows
Its frosty pepper up my nose.

Black are my steps on silver sod;
Thick blows my frosty breath abroad;
And tree and house, and hill and lake,
Are frosted like a wedding-cake.

Robert Louis Stevenson

Alone at Christmas

In December, 1977, John Helms caught the lift to the eighty-sixth floor of the Empire State Building in New York. The huge skyscraper towers over the streets of the city and Helms decided it was just right for what he had in mind.

'Nearly Christmas, I've got no money, no job, nobody cares about me,' thought the young artist, as the lift sped upwards. 'What's the good of it all?'

Minutes later he climbed over the safety fence round the observation platform and flung himself into space. He had decided that his life was no longer worth living.

Half an hour later John came to his senses. He was certainly not dead. He was not even hurt. As he had jumped from the eighty-sixth floor a strong gust of wind caught him and flung him onto a narrow window ledge – on the eighty-fifth floor!

'This is fantastic,' gasped John as he gazed down at the cars and people moving like toys and ants far below him. Suddenly the idea of committing suicide seemed dreadfully wrong. What had he been thinking about?

Meanwhile Bill Steckman was working in his office on the eighty-fifth floor. Sitting at his desk he felt the hairs on the back of his neck prickle with fright as he heard a tapping on the window.

'Nonsense,' he thought. 'Eighty-five floors up – who could be tapping on my window?'

He heard it again and, forcing himself to turn round, he almost fainted with shock as he saw a young man kneeling on the window ledge, tapping on the glass.

'Hold it, hold it,' breathed the astonished Steckman, as he moved to the window and hauled John to safety.

The story had a double happy ending. When details of it appeared in the newspapers people learned that John had been desperately lonely. At once hundreds of families contacted him and invited him to spend Christmas with them.

The holly tree's story

'Ah,' sighed the holly tree,' if only I didn't look such an unfriendly tree. My leaves are prickly until they go brown and die and I've got no fruit for people to come and enjoy. I wish somebody would give me a chance to show I can be as helpful as other trees.'

So thought the holly as it stood, rather lonely, a little way away from the other trees.

Then one night a cold and tired man came pushing into the wood.

'I've got to get some wood quickly! That new-born baby must be kept warm during the night.'

As he was in such a hurry he headed straight for the holly tree, which was the first one to take his eye. Shouldering its prickly leaves aside he pulled it from the ground and dragged it off behind him.

'Now to get back to that stable,' he thought. As soon as he reached the stable he chopped branches from the holly tree and made a fire. It blazed up quickly.

All through the long night the fire warmed the stable. Whenever its flames seemed in danger of dying down a small robin flew down from the roof and fanned them with its wings. Eventually the first light of dawn appeared and the exhausted bird flew back to the roof, its breast to remain red for ever after its work over the fire.

The man and woman sat staring into what was left of the fire. The baby slept soundly.

'Joseph,' said Mary, 'that fire has been wonderful. It has kept our baby warm all night.'

'You're right,' replied the man, smiling at his wife, and poking at what remained of the glowing red embers.

So the holly tree had been given a chance to prove how it could be helpful. From that moment onwards it became as special as the night during which Jesus was born. Its leaves remained shiny, green and bright all the year round, and the tree glows with red berries which look just like the embers which had glowed in the fire. What is more, the holly was no longer left alone and untouched in the woods. Since then it has been used to decorate homes and to remind people of that very first Christmas.

Wassailing Song

Wisselton, wasselton, who lives here?
We've come to taste your Christmas beer.
Up the kitchen and down the hall,
Holly, ivy and mistletoe;
A peck of apples will serve us all,
Give us some apples and let us go.

Up with your stocking, on with your shoe,
If you haven't any apples, money will do.
My carol's done, and I must be gone,
No longer can I stay here.
God bless you all, great and small,
And send you a happy new year.

(Traditional)

A catalogue of disaster

'What does Julie want for Christmas this year?' asked Albert Frost as he walked towards the bulldozer.

'A kitten – she won't hear of anything else,' replied Jim Mellowship.

The two men were about to start their morning's work. They were helping to redevelop an old hotel. The hotel had stood on its present site for hundreds of years, and now it was being altered and modernised.

'Funny thing about cats,' went on Albert. 'I was reading about them the other night. Did you know that in times past they were used to keep away evil spirits?'

'That sounds like a lot of rubbish to me,' replied Jim. 'How were they supposed to do that then?'

'Well, apparently, when a cat died its body was buried in or near a building. It kept away evil spirits.'

'Hmmm,' muttered Jim as Albert clambered up into the driving seat of the bulldozer.

Half an hour later work on the site was in full swing when the lifting of a great scoop of earth revealed a strange sight. A collection of small bones lay bared. They had obviously been undisturbed for a very long time.

Work stopped whilst the men looked at them.

'Well we can't stand looking at them all day lads,' said the foreman. 'Lift them out carefully and put them in the old stable block over there.'

Albert Frost nodded to Jim Mellowship as this was being done.

'Remember what I was telling you,' he said. 'That's a cat's skeleton that is.'

Albert was right. An expert was called in and he said that the mysterious collection of bones was the 300-year old skeleton of a cat.

'I bet it was put there to keep away evil spirits,' muttered Albert when he heard this news.

The rest of the men jeered at this until strange and frightening things began to happen. First of all the building company which was redeveloping the hotel ran into all sorts of difficulties. Finally the company had no money left. It went bankrupt and the work on the hotel stopped.

Next, the stable block where the cat's remains had been placed, mysteriously caught fire one night. The building was completely destroyed – but the bones survived undamaged. They were taken to a farmhouse which was close by. A few nights later the farmhouse burned to the ground, and again the bones were unharmed!

By now a new building company was preparing to start work on the project.

'There is something funny about the remains of this cat,' said the manager of the new company. 'I'm going to take them back to that hotel site to be on the safe side.'

However, as he was driving to the site with the bones in his car, he was involved in a serious crash. At exactly the same time the new roof which was being put on the hotel collapsed and fell in. Next, some beams which had recently been fixed unaccountably moved and caused another accident.

By now the builders were very worried indeed.

'We're just going to have to try and go back to the beginning and put this right,' said the new manager.

The local vicar was contacted and asked if he would say a burial service over the terrifying remains of the cat. This was done, and the bones were re-buried in a tiny coffin. In the coffin was a written note apologizing for the trouble it had been caused.

Work began again. This time there were no problems and the hotel has since turned out to be a happy and prosperous place.

(Based on a true story)

Especially for St Nicholas

In the year 1282 Archbishop Peckham of Canterbury decreed that 'the church of Esshe (Ashe), nearby Wingham, was constituted a parish and cure of souls.' The parish of Ashe still flourishes today, and the church of St Nicholas is the parish church (see p. 91 for details of St Nicholas' life).

In 1982 celebrations were held to mark the seven hundredth anniversary of the founding of the parish and a special service, attended by the Archbishop of Canterbury was held on St Nicholas' Day, 5 December. A hymn was written by two members of the congregation especially for this service. Here are the words of the hymn:

Hymn for St Nicholas

We sing thanks for the life
Of a Saint we hold dear,
For the life of a Saint
Bringing ev'ryone cheer.
We sing thanks to our Father
And praise to his Son
And remember Saint Nicholas,
His laughter and fun.

The fishermen and sailors,
As homeward they wend,
They rely on Saint Nicholas
As patron and friend.
In the wind and the storm,
Through the snow and the rain,
They think of Saint Nicholas
And comfort they gain.

We sing thanks for the life
Of a Saint we hold dear,
For the life of a Saint
Bringing ev'ryone cheer.

Fond legends and stories
Have often been told
Of the Bishop of Myra
Who shared all his gold.
How in dead of the night

To the chimneys he stole,
To rescue three maidens
With gifts of his gold.

We sing thanks for the life
Of a Saint we hold dear,
For the life of a Saint
Bringing ev'ryone cheer.

Each Christmas Eve at bedtime,
Our socks hung by the fire,
All our giving and sharing
This Saint does inspire.
For his kindliness to all
And his gifts to the poor,
For his wisdom and justice,
He's loved evermore.

We sing thanks for the life
Of a Saint we hold dear,
For the life of a Saint
Bringing ev'ryone cheer.
We sing thanks to our Father
And praise to his Son,
And remember Saint Nicholas,
His laughter and fun.

Jennie Bowen

Cherry tree carol

As Joseph was a-walking
He heard an angel sing:
'This night shall be the birth-time
Of Christ the heavenly king.

He neither shall be bornèd
In housen nor in hall,
Nor in a place of paradise
But in an ox's stall . . .'

(Anon)

A Christmas scene

The house fronts looked black enough, and the windows blacker, contrasting with the smooth white sheet of snow upon the roofs, and with the dirtier snow upon the ground; which last deposit had been ploughed up in deep furrows by the heavy wheels of carts and waggons; furrows that crossed and re-crossed each other hundreds of times where the great streets branched off; and made intricate channels, hard to trace in the thick yellow mud and icy water. The sky was gloomy, and the shortest streets were choked up with a dingy mist, half thawed, half frozen, whose heavier particles descended in a shower of sooty atoms, as if all the chimneys in Great Britain had, by one consent, caught fire, and were blazing away to their dear heart's content. There was nothing very cheerful in the climate or the town, and yet there was an air of cheerfulness abroad that the clearest summer air and brightest summer sun might have endeavoured to diffuse in vain.

For the people who were shovelling away on the house-tops were jovial and full of glee; calling out to one another from the parapets, and now and then exchanging a facetious snowball – better natured missile far than many a wordy jest – laughing heartily if it went wrong. The poulterers' shops were still half open, and the fruiterers' were radiant in their glory. There were great round, pot-bellied baskets of chestnuts, shaped like the waistcoats of jolly old gentlemen lolling at the doors, and tumbling out into the street in their apoplectic opulence. There were ruddy, brown-faced, brown-girthed Spanish onions, shining in the fatness of their growth like Spanish friars, and winking from their shelves in wanton slyness at the girls as they went by and glanced demurely at the hung-up mistletoe. There were pears and apples, clustered high in blooming pyramids; there were bunches of grapes, made in the shop-keepers' benevolence to dangle from conspicuous hooks, that people's mouths might water gratis as they passed; there were piles of filberts, mossy and brown, recalling, in their fragrance, ancient walks among the woods, and pleasant shufflings ankle-deep through withered leaves; there were Norfolk Biffins, squab and swarthy, setting off the yellow of the oranges and lemons, and, in the great compactness of their juicy persons, urgently entreating and beseeching to be carried home in paper bags and eaten after dinner. The very gold and silver fish, set forth among these choice fruits in a bowl, though members of a dull and stagnant-blooded race, appeared to know that there was something going on; and, to a fish, went gasping round and round their little world in slow and passionless excitement.

From *A Christmas Carol*, Charles Dickens

Christmas dinner

We were all sitting round the table.
There was roast turkey
there were roast potatoes
there were roast parsnips
there were broccoli tips
there was a dishful of crispy bacon off the turkey
there was wine, cider, lemonade
and milk for the youngsters.
Everything was set.
It was all on the table.
We were ready to begin.
Suddenly there was a terrible terrible scream.
Right next to the turkey was a worm.
A dirty little worm wriggling about like mad.

For a moment everyone looked at it.
Someone said very quietly, 'Oh dear.'
And everyone was thinking things like –
'How did it get there?'
'If it came out of that turkey,
I don't want any of it.'
or
'I'm not eating any Christmas dinner. It could be full of
dirty wriggly worms.'

Now – as it happens,
I don't mind wriggly worms.
There was plenty of room for it
at the table. It was just that . . . that . . .
no-one had asked it to come over
for Christmas dinner.

So I said,
'I don't think it came out of the turkey. I think –
it came off the bottom of the milk bottle.'
And I picked up the worm,
and put it out the door to spend Christmas day
in a lovely patch of wet mud.
Much nicer place to be –
for a worm.

Michael Rosen

Sam and the midnight music

Sam had never been so tired. He was used to being tired, for he was a very hard working boy. Bethlehem, where he lived, was a busy little town and the inn which his father and mother kept was the best run in that town, always full of visitors wanting beds and food, fodder for their animals and directions to the next city. His mother and father worked hard, too, so when Sam's big brothers and his bossy sister Ruth were tired, they all took it out on Sam. Sam was used to being tired.

But tonight was different. Tonight was the ending of the busiest day in Sam's life. People had come to Bethlehem from all over the country to be counted and registered by the Roman soldiers who were stamping in squads through the narrow streets. Some of the people had arrived early and taken all the rooms in the inn, but as more and more families streamed into the courtyard clamouring for a place to sleep, Sam's father began to pack his guests in more tightly. Sam and his brothers had to hump sleeping mats, fetch extra food and hay, break it to furious guests that they would be sleeping with six or eight others, even do the girls' jobs of bringing more water from the well because their mother and Ruth could not be spared from the kitchen.

It was now long after dark. Sam ached in every bone. His head was spinning. His foot ached where a donkey had trodden on it, and his ear burned where his brother John had clouted it. He dropped on to a bundle of hay and sat there, watching the chain of lanterns and torches winding up the hill as still more people came crowding into Bethlehem. The stars were cold and brilliant; one hung low above the inn, clear as a diamond. Sam huddled back into the hay and hoped that no-one would notice him.

Then he realised that a separate little commotion was going on, quite apart from the general noise and crush. Something was happening in the stable at the end of the yard. His mother shot out of the kitchen with a pile of towels and a steaming bowl; a man was shouting; his brothers were turning away other guests who wanted to tie up their beasts. For a moment the stable was the centre of the world – and over it all the great star shone and a strange thrilling expectation, like music, filled the midnight air. The whole yard, the whole town, the black hills beyond – they were all brimming with this sense of splendour and excitement.

Sam got to his weary legs. He had to go and see what was happening. He took two steps towards the stable – when he heard someone very close beside him. Someone was crying. It was a small, muffled wail and he nearly missed it. He peered round the bundle of hay.

On the other side, squatting on the stones and curled into a ball, her thumb in her mouth, was a little girl. Big tears were running down her face. She seemed to be quite alone in all the crowd.

'What's up?' said Sam. 'Are you lost?'

The little girl nodded.

'I was with my mum, holding on to her skirt and someone pushed between us and – . . .'

She put her thumb abruptly back in her mouth and two more tears trickled down her dirty face.

'Well, we'll find your mum,' said Sam, with a confidence that he did not feel. 'What's her name? Where's she staying?'

'Rebecca,' said the girl. 'We were going to stay with my Uncle Ben. He's a potter.'

Sam's heart sank. Bethlehem was full of potters and at least three of them were called Ben.

'Come on,' he said, taking her warm, damp hand. 'I live in this town. I'll find your uncle.'

They pushed their way out into the narrow, crowded streets. Wriggling, ducking, dodging loaded camels and bewildered groups of newcomers, they ended up, bruised and breathless, on the doorstep of the nearest Ben the potter. Sam beat on the door.

'Go away!' shouted a voice from inside. 'There's no room here. Try the inn.'

'Have you got someone called Rebecca staying with you?' Sam shouted back.

'Certainly not! Will you go away and let me get some sleep?' roared the voice. A shutter hanged to and was bolted. The little girl gave a big, silent sob.

'It's all right,' said Sam, annoyed. 'We'll find her, don't worry.' He stood on the doorstep looking up and down the road – and saw, far away, a whole line of camels turning into his own inn yard. Even at that distance, he could tell from the servants, the bundles, the way that the crowd fell back, that this was a group of very rich customers. His father would be rushing round in a panic and certainly shouting for Sam. And now the air about him seemed to be fairly vibrating with the strange music. It called and called him . . . He swallowed hard, took the damp little hand again and set firmly off in the opposite direction.

A squad of Roman soldiers came swinging down the street, nearly trampling them flat. They passed with a clatter and a swirl of cloaks as Sam and the girl slithered into the doorway of the second Ben the potter. Just as they arrived the door opened. A frantic-looking women peered out. The girl gave a shriek of 'Mum!' and hurled herself at the woman. Sam, not waiting to be thanked, set off back up the street. Going home was even worse, for he was now pushing against the crowd, and the music was fading with the stars. He fell over feet, bumped into a fat lady, was cursed by an old man – and finally crawled into the inn yard in the thin grey light of dawn just in time to have his ear seized and gripped by his big sister Ruth. (It was his sore ear!)

'And where do you think you've been?' she shouted. 'Going off just when you're needed, you lazy little pest! All the trouble we've had with those people in the stable – the woman having a baby, and a gang of no-good shepherds coming from the hills with their horrible dogs, and then the noblemen from heaven knows where with their camels and none of their servants able to understand a word we said – '

Sam ducked under her arm and ran for the stable, leaving her complaining into space.

It was so quiet inside that he stood dazed, taking time to get used to the darkness and peace. He could hear the beasts munching . . . and the hay rustling as someone turned over . . . Yes, there were two people lying on the hay, asleep. And from the stone manger, filled with dry grass, came the tiny whimpering crow of a very new baby.

One of the sleepers stirred and sat up. It was a young woman. Sam could see her face, white and smiling, in the dawn light through the open door. 'I missed it all,' he said, 'I wanted to come and see what the music was about, and all the people, and I missed it. But I had to find the little girl's mum for her, didn't I?'

'You did the best thing of all,' said the woman. 'The very best thing. The shepherds brought my little son presents for a shepherd, and he is going to be a shepherd. The kings brought him presents for a king, and he is going to be a king. You have brought him the present of a helping hand, to warm his heart and welcome him into this hard world. Thank you.'

Sam bent his head awkwardly, smiled back at her and at the sleeping baby, and went out. Ruth was standing, glaring, in the yard. Sam gave her a huge friendly grin, picked up a brush and began to sweep the dirty stones. Ruth grinned too. 'Young monkey!' she said, quite kindly, and went in. Sam went on brushing; after a bit he started to whistle.

Pamela Egan

I Saw Three Ships

I saw three ships come sailing in,
On Christmas Day, on Christmas Day,
I saw three ships come sailing in,
On Christmas Day in the morning.

And what was in those ships all three?
On Christmas Day, on Christmas Day,
And what was in those ships all three?
On Christmas Day in the morning.

Our Saviour Christ and his lady,
On Christmas Day, on Christmas Day,
Our Saviour Christ and his lady,
On Christmas Day in the morning.

Pray, whither sailed those ships all three?
On Christmas Day, on Christmas Day,
Pray, whither sailed those ships all three?
On Christmas Day in the morning.

O, they sailed into Bethlehem,
On Christmas Day, on Christmas Day,
O, they sailed into Bethlehem,
On Christmas Day in the morning.

(Traditional)

Who was Good King Wenceslas?

In the city of Prague, in Czechoslovakia, there is a large square with the statue of a young man in it. The square is called Wenceslas Square and the writing beneath the statue says: 'Saint Wenceslas suffer not us nor our children to perish.' The fact that the statue is of a young man tells its own rather sad story . . .

Wenceslas was born in Czechoslovakia over a thousand years ago. Although his father, the king, was a Christian, his mother was not. When Wenceslas was twelve his father died and, as he was too young to be king, his mother ruled the country. She brought in heathen nobles to help her do this and Wenceslas was sent off to live with his grandmother, Ludmilla.

Ludmilla was a Christian and she taught Wenceslas about Christianity and the need to care for other people. The nobles at court heard about this and recognised how dangerous it could be for them.

'Your majesty,' said one of the nobles to the queen, 'Ludmilla is poisoning your son's mind.'

'Yes,' said another, 'we've got to do something about it or we'll have a revolt on our hands.'

'Hmmmm,' answered the queen, and the nobles were quick to take advantage of her hesitation.

'Leave it to us your majesty,' said the first noble, 'we'll sort out the problem for you.'

'Very well,' replied the queen.

The nobles took action immediately. The noblemen rode off to Ludmilla's castle. They found the old woman in her chapel – and they murdered her there.

Wenceslas was horrified but there was nothing he could do – at the moment. When he had got over the shock of his grandmother's death Wenceslas was surer than ever that what he had learned from her was something he ought to know even more about. So he began to smuggle Christian priests into the castle to help him learn more about Christian teachings. He also asked them to teach him how to read and write.

By the time he was eighteen, and old enough to be king, Wenceslas knew exactly what he wanted. First he banished his mother and her cruel and murderous nobles from court. Then he set about organising a strong and loyal army which would protect his people from invading tribes. Then he made sure that children were as well looked after and educated as possible.

All the while however his enemies, the nobles, were plotting against him. They were delighted to find that Boleslav, Wenceslas's brother was jealous of the king's popularity with his people.

'With him out of the way, you would be the king!' said one of the nobles. 'Not only that, you would be every bit as popular as he is. Some people might even thank you for getting him out of the way.'

The weak and envious Boleslav allowed himself to be persuaded by the nobles, and a treacherous plot was arranged.

'Brother,' said Boleslav one day to Wenceslas, 'I'm sorry to have behaved so badly towards you. I have been foolish and jealous. Let me make it up to you. Come and stay with me at my castle for a few days and let us learn how to be friends again.'

Wenceslas was delighted. He had always been sorry Boleslav was so much against him.

'What a marvellous idea,' he said, and so a date for the visit was arranged. When the time came, and Wenceslas arrived at his brother's castle, Boleslav met him with open arms.

'Let us go to the chapel I have had specially prepared,' said Boleslav.

'Of course,' replied Wenceslas, pleased that his brother was obviously thinking of becoming a Christian too.

So the two men walked arm in arm to the chapel. Once there, they stepped inside – and then Wenceslas heard bolts being slammed in the door behind him. Turning, he saw three nobles standing there with daggers drawn. He knew at once that he had been tricked, but it was too late. At the age of twenty-two the much-loved king was murdered by the treacherous friends of his brother.

Christmas parcels!

Christmas parcels have always been exciting things to receive, but the relation of cost and contents has changed considerably over the years.

The following description of Christmas parcels comes from an advertisement which appeared in a magazine called 'Illustrated Bits' in 1886.

'Look. Look. Look. Grand monster Santa Claus surprise parcels. Each parcel contains: 12 very handsome and choice Christmas and New Year Cards of new and original designs; 4 beautifully coloured Christmas mottoes suitable for decorations; 1 fine silver plated thimble, enamelled inside; 1 fine steel pocket knife with bone handle; 1 leatherette writing case and companion (everybody needs this); 1 bijou draught board and set of draughts; 1 24-note celestial tone harmonica; 1 book of *Language of the Flowers*; Precious Stones; 1 gold plated representation Spade Guinea suitable for watch charm or pendant; 1 gold or silver plated stem winding toy, watch charm or chain – the child's delight; 1 magic frog or spider; 1 universal patent mechanograph; pictures; designs; maps; plans; 1 child's nursery tale book . . . Just think . . . we will send the entire parcel post paid to any address in the UK for 2s 9d, two parcels for 5s 3d or three parcels for 7s 6d.'

One good turn deserves another

In the British Isles Christmas is the time for thoughtful present giving. In Japan, New Year is the time for presents. The following story indicates that the ideals however remain the same . . .

. . . Yosaku put down the hat that he was weaving. He looked across at his wife who was still hard at work on hers.

'I would like to get two rice cakes so that we could celebrate New Year properly,' thought the old man to himself as he looked at his wife's tired face. 'My dear wife works so hard but we seem to stay so very poor.'

Yosaku's wife suddenly looked up and caught her husband looking at her. She smiled.

'I know what you are thinking Yosaku,' she said. 'New Year's Day is the day after tomorrow and we haven't any rice cakes. Don't worry, when we've finished these two hats we'll have five ready to sell. That will give us some money to buy the rice cakes.'

Next morning Yosaku got up early because it was a very long walk to town. He looked out of the window and saw thick snow everywhere.

'Oh dear,' he thought, 'that will make it harder to get to town and there will be fewer people about to buy the hats.'

Yosaku was right. After making the long journey to town he found he could not sell one single hat. Disappointed and hungry he set off to return home.

'No money – no rice cakes,' he thought, 'my poor wife will be so disappointed.'

On his way home Yosaku had to climb up a steep mountain path. By the side of the path were six stone statues of Jizo, the protector of children. When Yosaku reached the statues he saw that every one of them was covered with snow.

'That doesn't seem right,' he muttered. 'Even the statue of somebody who cares for children should be kept as warm as possible.'

The old man swept the snow away from the statues. Then, looking at the sky which was still tumbling snowflakes, he gave a sigh and put one of his straw hats on the head of one of the statues. Going along the row he covered five stone heads with his fine straw hats.

'That will keep them much warmer,' he said. Then of course he realised that there were six statues, and he only had five hats.

'No problem at all,' he thought, and took off his own hat and put it on the sixth statue.

Some hours later he reached home. His wife, who had been getting rather worried about him, was looking out of the window. As soon as Yosaku reached the door she opened it and welcomed him inside.

'You look frozen,' she said. 'Your head is soaking wet. You are not a young man any more you know, you must take more care. Come and sit beside the fire whilst I get you some warm food.'

'I have only bad news, wife,' the old man said miserably. 'I bring back no money – and no rice cakes.'

'Aaah,' replied his wife, 'you are here, that is the important thing.'

Yosaku sat by the fire, got warm and ate his hot food, he told his wife the whole story. Far from being angry, she smiled when he had finished, and there was just a glint of tears in her eyes.

'Oh Yosaku, that was a lovely thought of yours. If we had been lucky enough to have children of our own we would have wanted Jizo looked after.'

By now darkness had long fallen. Tired, and rather hungry, the two old people went to bed. Outside the night was cold and bleak. Just before dawn Yosaku was awakened by a strange noise.

'What is that?' he thought, and listened carefully.

'It can't be . . . but it is . . . it is someone singing!'

Waking his wife up, they both listened. It was somebody singing, and the only word of the song they could pick out clearly was 'Jizo.' Then, as suddenly as it had started, the singing stopped.

'Let's go and see what is happening out there,' said Yosaku. So the two old people tiptoed to the door and opened it wide.

'Look. . . .' gasped Yosaku.

'I don't believe it,' whispered his wife.

Both of them were looking at the step outside their door. Someone had spread a large mat on it and on the mat was the biggest, freshest, most beautiful rice cake either of them had ever seen.

'Who could have done this for us?' mumbled Yosaku.

'Look,' said his wife, pointing to the path which led to the woods and mountains, and which was now lit with the first lovely red light of dawn. There, tinted by the early light which was reflected off the snow were six stone figures. Each wore a straw hat and each was moving slowly towards the wood. The sound of singing could just be faintly heard coming from them.

'Jizo knew how kind you were,' said Yosaku's wife, squeezing his arm, 'and now he has sent us the most wonderful New Year's gift we have ever had.'

The two old people then lifted up the rice cake and carried it indoors.

(Adapted from an old Japanese folk tale)

Long Long Ago

Winds through the olive trees
Softly did blow,
Round little Bethlehem
Long, long ago.

Sheep on the hillside lay
Whiter than snow;
Shepherds were watching them,
Long, long ago.

Then from the happy sky,
Angels bent low,
Singing their songs of joy,
Long, long ago.

> For in a manger bed,
> Cradled we know,
> Christ came to Bethlehem
> Long, long ago.
>
> (Author unknown)

The lesson

The wind whistled round the turrets of the old castle and swirls of snow lashed against the shutters. In his small room at the top of the castle Rowland pulled a blanket round his shoulders and shivered.

'It wasn't always like this,' the old man thought. 'To think that I am treated worse than a servant and in my own home.'

Rowland thought back over the years to how his present state had come about. He remembered when he was a young man and a shrewd merchant. Shrewd enough to make a lot of money buying and selling things. Shrewd enough to buy this splendid castle for his family to live in.

'Ah,' he thought to himself. 'How happy Marie and I were in those days, and how pleased we were when we knew we were to have a child.'

A gust of wind rattled the shutters and Rowland's face darkened as he remembered how that keenly awaited moment had turned to tragedy. Marie and he had had a fine son – but his beloved wife died giving birth to the child.

'Still,' murmured Rowland, 'he was a fine son. How he could wrestle and ride like the wind . . . and he knew how to work too. I was right to give him the castle and all my wealth while he was still a young man.'

Rowland thought back to the time Mark, his son, had taken over all his possessions.

'It's best this way father,' Mark had said. 'I'll carry on the business and you can live here in your lovely old castle without any worries at all. You deserve such a life.'

For a time it had been a splendid life. Rowland rode his brown mare, visited his friends, wore his fine cloaks . . . and then Mark got married.

His wife was the daughter of a noble who lived nearby. The noble was a foolish and extravagant man, and he was glad to be rid of his daughter because it meant he had one less mouth to feed. Edwina was beautiful, but because she came from a noble family she was very proud and full of her own importance.

'That old man will have to be moved to a room in the attic,' she said to Mark one day. 'He is always getting in the way.'

'But he is my father,' protested Mark.

'That may be,' went on Edwina, 'but he doesn't do anything does he? I mean he doesn't work or anything now does he? No – to the attic with him.'

So the years went by. Rowland grew older and felt more and more neglected. There was only one bright spark in the old man's life. Mark and Edwina had a son, Peter, and as he grew up he and his grandfather became great friends. Edwina disapproved of course, but whenever he could, Peter crept upstairs to talk to the old man.

Now, it was nearly Christmas and Rowland thought, with a smile, of the fine knife he had treasured for years.

'It will be Peter's Christmas present this year,' he said to himself.

At that moment there was a clatter outside the door and, to Rowland's surprise, his son Mark entered.

'Mark,' he said, 'how nice to see you. Sit down my boy.'

'I'm sorry father,' Mark blurted out, 'but you are going to have to go.'

'Go,' gasped the old man. 'Go . . . go where?'

'Edwina is having a ball here in the castle tomorrow night – Christmas Eve. We'll need all the rooms for her friends to stay in. So she thought as you would have to move out for one night, you might as well move for good. It would be far better for you if you found somewhere to live in the village anyway. Please pack your things and be ready to go tomorrow.'

Before Rowland had a chance to reply his son hurried out of the room.

The old man spent a miserable night. The next morning he was up early to pack his few belongings. As he was doing so the door opened and his grandson Peter came in.

'Ah, I'm glad to see you,' said Rowland. 'I was going to give this to you as a Christmas present, but as I have to leave today I'd like you to have it now.'

He gave Peter the beautiful old knife with the ivory handle.

'Thank you,' said the boy simply, and left.

Disappointed that the boy could find nothing else to say, or more time to stay with him, Rowland shouldered his pack, gathered up his one last thick coat, and went downstairs.

Mark, Edwina and Peter were in the great hall by a blazing fire.

'You'll be all right father,' said Mark in a falsely cheerful voice. 'You'll soon find somewhere to live.'

Rowland could find nothing to say. He walked slowly towards the door, and then Peter's voice stopped him.

'Grandfather!' called Peter, and Rowland was surprised at the harsh way he said it.

'Let me have your coat for a minute,' went on the boy.

Surprised, Rowland handed him the coat, and was astonished when Peter took out the knife he had been given as his Christmas present and, with a quick stroke, slashed the coat in half. Then he threw one half of the coat to his grandfather, and put the other half under his arm.

For a moment there was a shocked silence, and Rowland felt tears prick his eyes at this last, and most hurtful, treatment. Then Mark bellowed.

'What on earth did you do that for? How dare you do that to your grandfather?'

Peter replied at once.

'Well father, I have watched how you and mother have treated grandfather. That was a very good coat he had so I thought I would take half of it. Then when you get old, and I order you out of my home, I will give you this half.'

There was another, even longer silence. It was broken when Mark suddenly stepped forward to his father.

'How can you ever forgive me?' he said, 'Please stay and let me try to put right the wrongs I have done you.'

Then Edwina was beside Rowland too.

'It was not really Mark's fault father,' she said. 'It was mine. I've been selfish and thoughtless. Please choose the room you would most like to live in and we'll have your things put there immediately and . . . will you be our guest of honour at the Christmas Ball tonight?'

The three turned and made their way back to the fire where Peter stood. All looked at him and said just three words, 'Thank you Peter.'

(Based on an old French folk tale)

Father Christmas aliases

Whilst everybody immediately recognises 'Santa Claus' and 'Father Christmas' as names associated with Christmas, there are different Christmas figures in other parts of the world.

The Sharman, for instance, was a mysterious midwinter visitor in places such as Siberia and North America. North American Indians recognised him as a sort of witch doctor who could be asked to look after their welfare. The Sharman was also associated with the reindeer, and Sharman sticks were put up through the smoke holes of tents during the midwinter feasts. The strange links between a figure riding the skies, reindeers and entry through chimneys can be seen here.

Sinter Klaas is still a very significant figure in Holland. He arrives in Amsterdam on 6 December with Piet, his Moorish helper, and leads a procession along the old canals. Great crowds welcome his arrival. In Germany there is the Christkindl (Christ child) who leaves Christmas presents on Christmas Eve, and Knecht Rupprecht who is aware of all naughty behaviour. In Finland the name for the giver of presents is Joulupukki, and in Iceland there are several – a group of goblins known as Jola Steinar. The significant figure in Italy is Befana, who is associated with Epiphany. Not only does she distribute presents then but she supposedly directed the Wise Men to Bethlehem. The Russian Father Christmas is 'Grandfather Frost' who delivers presents with the help of the Snow Maiden. In Norway the Christmas gnome Julenisse has to have a bowl of porridge put out for him so that he is persuaded not to do any mischief in the houses he visits.

Dick Whittington – fact or fiction?

Chapter 7 in this book – 'Behind the Scenes at a Pantomime' – describes a production of 'Dick Whittington.' One of the most memorable features of any such pantomime is 'the Cat.' Its place in Dick's life story however seems to be mainly fictional.

Dick was not born in poverty, his father was Sir William Whittington of Gloucestershire. In 1371, when Dick was 13, he went to London to serve an apprenticeship with Sir Ivor Fitzwarren, a distant relation of his mother and a rich merchant adventurer.

Dick was not only successful himself, but he married Alice Fitzwarren and inherited her father's fortune. As one of the richest men in London he used his money in such a way as to make himself very popular. For a start he lent money to the kings who were on the throne during his lifetime, and he bought the wedding dresses used by Henry IV's daughters. He also paid for St Bartholomew's hospital to be restored, and was very generous to the poor. He was Lord Mayor of London three times – 1397–8; 1406–7; 1419–20.

When Dick died in 1423 his fortune was left to charity as he had no children of his own. Some of the money went towards the rebuilding of Newgate prison and improving the conditions for the prisoners.

But what about 'the Cat'? The first linking of Dick with a cat was in a ballad which appeared in 1605. Various romantic suggestions of how the cat came into his life have been made over the years, but the reality seems to have been very dull and ordinary. Much of Whittington's fortune was made by trading in coal, and the old north-eastern name for a sailing ship which carried the coal to London was – a Cat!

'Gordon Bennett!'

Christmas is often a time of surprises. There are unexpected presents, unexpected visitors, and people often do unexpectedly kind things. For many years some people have used a very strange expression when they get a surprise. They gasp, 'Gordon Bennett!'

The reason this expression came into being was because the real Gordon Bennett was a man who became famous for the surprising things he did. He was an American who was born in New York in 1841 and he became the very rich owner of a newspaper called *The New York Herald*.

Seeing how desperately poor and in need many people were in some parts of New York, he arranged for free kitchens to provide food for them. He also gave one hundred thousand dollars for other kinds of help.

For some of his life, however, Gordon Bennett lived in Paris and it was one December there when he produced one of his greatest surprises . . .

'What is your name sir?' asked the waiter.

'My name is Gordon Bennett,' replied the man, 'but what has that got to do with you?'

'I am afraid,' said the waiter, 'that we have only got tables for those people who have made reservations. Unfortunately your name is not on our list of reservations.'

Gordon Bennett paused for a moment and then said angrily.

'Where can I find the owner?'

'But sir, he won't be able to help. There are just no . . .'

'The owner!'

Soon Bennett was being shown into the owner's office. The waiter explained the situation and the owner shrugged his shoulders.

'How can I help you sir? You heard what the waiter said.'

'I want to buy this restaurant,' replied Gordon Bennett. 'How much will you sell it to me for?'

The owner looked at the waiter and lifted his eyebrows. Obviously they were dealing with a madman here. Still, why not have a joke about it?

'Very well,' he replied, 'the restaurant is yours for one million francs.'

Without a moment's hesitation Gordon Bennett replied, 'It's a deal.'

Then to the owner's absolute astonishment, he reached into his pocket and brought out a million francs in large notes. Placing them on the owner's desk he spoke again.

'I believe I now own a restaurant. Be good enough to give me the deeds to this place.'

The surprises, however, were far from over.

'Kindly prepare a table for me at once,' Bennett said to the open-mouthed waiter, 'and I will want my favourite meal.'

Expecting some spectacular order the waiter paused before Bennett added, 'That will be mutton chops.'

An hour later Gordon Bennett sat at his table, an empty plate in front of him. He called the waiter over to him.

'That was a splendid meal,' he said. 'From now on I want you to make sure that there is always a table reserved for me, whether it is Christmas or Midsummer's Day. Please make sure you always have mutton chops on the menu for me too.'

'Of course sir,' said the waiter.

'Oh, and by the way,' went on Bennett, 'you are the new owner of this restaurant.'

So saying he took the deeds of the restaurant out of his pocket and handed them to the flabbergasted waiter. This must have been one of the most sensational and surprising Christmas presents there has ever been!

A ghost story – with a difference

Children love eerie stories and the dark, gloomy afternoons of December are ideal times for telling them. If a frightening story can be supplemented by a visual aid then this is a marvellous bonus. What follows here therefore are details of the 'visual aid' and how it can be prepared beforehand. Then comes the story which will reveal naturally how the 'aid' can be used – and the necessity for the storyteller to keep his hand in his pocket whilst telling the tale!

A further suggestion is for the teacher to read the story first and then re-tell it, rather than simply reading it aloud.

Preparation of the visual aid – The Missing Finger!
Materials required: a matchbox, a razor blade, cotton wool, talcum powder or flour, a 'darkening agent' such as black magic marker, charcoal or eye make-up, 'blood' – eg, red ink, tomato ketchup.

Technique
1   Cut a hole in the bottom of the matchbox drawer. This must be large enough for the storyteller's finger to go through.
2   Prepare a 'ghostly' finger by coating it in flour or talcum powder, 'bruising' the nail by turning it black with the 'darkening agent.'
3   Spread the cotton wool round the hole in the matchbox drawer and stain it with 'blood'.
4   Insert finger through hole and lay it alongside the blood-stained cotton wool. Slide the outside cover of the matchbox over the drawer part so that the top of the finger is hidden. When cupped in hand, the ghostly finger appears to be lying in the matchbox.
5   Remember that whilst the story is being told the hand containing the matchbox and the 'finger' should be kept in the storyteller's pocket, ready to be produced with a flourish at the denouement of the following story . . .

Figure 1

The missing finger

When does fun turn to bullying? It's hard to know I suppose, but I'll never forget that Christmas when it all started with a bit of teasing . . .

We were out in the woods, miles from anywhere, collecting holly and mistletoe to take back for decorations. There'd been the usual mucking about, snowball throwing and the like, and then Darren, who was the oldest, yelled, 'Let's leave Peter in the woods.'

Well, I'm Peter and the others were all older than me. I never thought they'd do it, but I was wrong. Charging through the powdery snow they ran off into the gathering gloom. I couldn't keep up with them and suddenly I found myself alone.

The distant shouts and jeers died away and I was left standing there. My breath billowed out in front of me, icicles glistened sharply in the trees, and there was silence.

At first I wasn't much bothered but then a feeling of panic began to creep over me. I didn't know the woods at all, I had no idea where the path out was, it was getting dark, it was . . .

'Keep calm, keep calm,' I said to myself. Lifting one foot out of the snow I followed it with the other and began to walk slowly in the direction which Darren and the others had taken. I suppose I must have been walking for about ten minutes when I saw it. There, hidden amongst the trees, with apparently no path leading to it stood an old, rather tumbledown-looking cottage. At first I thought it was deserted, but then I noticed the flickering of a candle in the window.

'At least they'll be able to direct me,' I thought and stumbled through the snow to the door. It had great iron bars across it and seemed to be made of terrifically heavy wood. I gave a hesitant knock.

Nothing happened. I knocked again. The light seemed to flicker away from the window, as if someone had picked it up to come to the door. There was the sound of heavy bolts being slid back and with a creak, the door opened slightly. A woman peered out.

'Yes?'

'I'm lost', I said. 'Could you tell me how to get to Frampton . . . or could I use your telephone . . . or . . .'

I faltered, and then shrugged helplessly. The woman put her head out of the door and looked around to see if there was anybody else about. She was neither young nor old, but her face had a dry, parchment look about it. She was very pale and her large eyes seemed both strained and sad.

'Come in,' she said, in a hollow-sounding voice. I stepped inside and the huge door closed behind me. The room I stood in was dull and old fashioned. Dust lay over heavy stuffed armchairs and as the woman moved towards a table with the candle I could see that it carried plates and mugs which did not seem to have been washed for years.

'You're lost?' she said, pushing back a wisp of hair.

'Yes, my friends ran off and left me and . . .'

'I know what,' she said, interrupting me, 'I'll go for help.'

'But . . . all I want to know . . .'

'No, no,' she went on – and her whole face came alive with something like excitement and relief, 'I'll go quickly, I'll go now . . . he never comes down anymore . . . nobody will know I've . . .'

Almost desperate with this strange excitement and impatience she dragged an old shawl from the back of a chair and hurried to the door. Before I could say another word she was gone.

I stood speechless in the musty room. For the second time in just half an hour I felt alone and frightened. Why had she rushed out – and where to? I just didn't understand.

I looked at the flickering candle – and then I heard it. The groan was low, and it had a half human, half animal sound about it. I felt the hair on the back of my neck prickle with terror. Then I heard the first footstep.

Rooted to the spot I heard the groans get louder, mixed with a curious panting noise. A second and third footstep sounded on the stairs and a strange dragging noise accompanied them. They grew nearer and nearer to the door at the back of the room. Then, the final terror, a puff of wind blew out the candle!

With a scream I suddenly found my voice and movements. Hurling myself towards the heavy door I flung it open and made to dash out. In my haste I caught my sleeve on the latch and, pulling it free, I was just too late to get my hand out of the way of the closing door. A terrible pain shot through my finger and up my arm. Ignoring it as best I could I ploughed through the snow, desperate to get away from . . . I didn't know what.

It must have been some hours later when I woke up, sweating and feverish. I was in hospital. Darren and the others had come back to look for me, and I had been lying unconscious in the snow. Now I was in hospital, with a heavily bandaged hand.

When I told my story, nobody believed me. There was no cottage . . . I had obviously hurt my hand in a fall . . . I would soon be better . . . it would just take a little time . . .

After a few days I was allowed out of hospital. Lying in bed in my own home the next morning I heard the postman walk up the path and ring the bell. For no reason a feeling of terror swept over me . . . it was as if I was back in the cottage . . . but why . . .?

I went downstairs and opened the door.

'Package for you,' said the postman, handing me a small box with my name on it.

'Thank you,' I gasped and closed the door behind him. My heart pounded and my mouth went dry as I tore off the wrapping. A cry burst from my lips as I saw . . .

(Now produce the match box!)

Chapter 3

A Christmas occasion

The main aim of this chapter is to present a 'Christmas Occasion' which can readily be adapted for use with almost any age group. The service/dramatic activity suggested here is not very original, but the framework of it is such that teachers can alter and adapt almost any part of it to suit their particular needs.

At the conclusion of the text provided there is a list of further sources suggesting recommended material to use with alternative presentations.

A Christmas occasion

Introductory carol for all   'Hark the Herald Angels Sing.'

NARRATOR	'We begin today with a scene which takes place in thousands of homes on Christmas morning. Let us imagine that we are taking a look at what is happening in Number 33 Everywhere Street . . . .'
DRAMA	A family is gathered round a Christmas tree. At the foot of the tree are some parcels. In the tree are some hidden crackers.
ANITA	'Look . . . let's get the crackers first . . . .'
DARREN	'. . . and pull them.'
ANITA	'I wonder what's in them?'
MUM	'You'll have to pull them and find out.'
DAD	'You might get a surprise.'

ANITA	'Come on Darren, let's pull one with each hand.' *(crackers are pulled with appropriate bangs)*
MUM	'What are the surprises?'
DARREN	'Here's a hat . . . and a false moustache.'
ANITA	'I've got a pair of trick glasses.'
DAD	*(looking among the parcels)* 'Here's another surprise – a parcel with my name on it!'
MUM	'Perhaps you'd better open it then.' *(Dad opens parcel – muttering about what he thinks it might be before he actually sees.)*
DAD	'Could it be . . . a book . . . a box of chocolates . . . a . . . NO! A video of great football matches – what a fantastic surprise!'
MUM	'Right, let's all open our parcels' *(The group opens parcels – making exclamations as they do so.)*
ANITA	'It's that great game we saw in Keddies!'
DARREN	'More gear for Action Man . . . terrific.'
MUM	'Oh Bill, you shouldn't have . . . it's too expensive . . . but what a marvellous surprise!'
DARREN	'I wish every morning was Christmas morning.'
MUM	'Yes, still, we must get cleared up now. Come on, tidy everything up.' *(Chatter, singing, etc., as group leaves the stage, taking away everything except the Christmas tree.)*
NARRATOR	'You will have noticed how often the word "surprise" was used in our play. Now we are going to leave Everywhere Street. We are going to go back in time nearly two thousand years, when some other people were getting a surprise. It wasn't the sort of surprise Mum, Dad, Anita and Darren got on Christmas morning. It was very different . . .'
DRAMA	A scene shows Joseph and Mary.
JOSEPH	'I'm sorry Mary, I never thought we'd have to go.'
MARY	'But do they know our baby is going to be born so soon?'

JOSEPH	'I don't suppose so, but it wouldn't make any difference. The Romans say we've got to go back to Bethlehem to register, so that's it.'
MARY	'When will we go?'
JOSEPH	'First thing tomorrow. At least I've got a donkey for you to ride on.'
MARY	'Will it take us long to get to Bethlehem?'
JOSEPH	'A few days.'
MARY	'I'm sure everything will be all right Joseph. Don't worry.'
JOSEPH	'I can't help worrying, my dear. It's a very long journey to Bethlehem and the place is sure to be crowded when we get there.'
MARY	'It will all work out without any trouble, you'll see.'
JOSEPH	'I hope you're right. This journey is a surprise we could have done without!' *(exit Joseph and Mary)*
CAROL	'Little Donkey' *(this could be sung by a choir; or a small group of children with simple percussion accompaniment; or everyone if desired)*
NARRATOR	'So Joseph and Mary had an unpleasant surprise. They had expected their baby to be born in the comfort of their own home. Instead they were faced with this frightening journey because the Romans said every man in the country had to go back to the town where he was born so that he could be registered. This was so that the Romans could be sure everyone would then pay the proper taxes. Many people had been born in Bethlehem but no longer lived there. Now they all went flooding back. Camps were set up outside the town and the streets were packed with crowds of people. This was what Mary and Joseph found when they arrived.'
DRAMA	A crowd scene – jostling, pushing, shouting. Included in the throng are Mary, Joseph, Beggar, Sweet salesman, Old man, Young woman, Roman soldier.
MARY	'I'm glad we left the donkey Joseph, we could never have got along this street.'

JOSEPH	'Yes, but you shouldn't be walking in crowds like this. We must find somewhere soon.'
BEGGAR	'I heard that. Oh yes you must. For a piece of silver I'll take you to just the place. Money first and then I'll take you . . .'
SWEET SALESMAN	'Pay no attention to him. Everywhere is full up. He can't get you in anywhere. What you need is a little something special to eat. I've got just the thing here . . .' *(Roman soldier pushes through the jostling, arguing crowd.)*
ROMAN SOLDIER	'Clear this street! Get out of my way you lot. Clear the street!'
YOUNG WOMAN	'Oh sir, sir – I've lost my husband. You haven't seen a tall, dark man wearing a . . .'
ROMAN SOLDIER	'Don't be silly, woman. There are thousands of people in these streets. Come on – clear the way.' *(Roman soldier pushes on.)*
OLD MAN	*(to Joseph)* 'Excuse me young man, I might be able to help.'
JOSEPH	'It would be marvellous if you could.'
OLD MAN	'There's a small inn just on the outskirts of the town. It's worth a try.'
MARY	'Oh, thank you – anything is worth a try!'
OLD MAN	'Keep on down this street and turn left at the end by the city wall. You'll come to it there.'
JOSEPH AND MARY	'Thank you.' *(exit the whole group)*
NARRATOR	'Mary and Joseph searched until they found the inn which the old man had described. It was an old, poor-looking place with some stables hollowed out of the rock beside which it stood. Holding Mary's hand, Joseph approached the door and gave a loud knock. When the landlord answered Joseph spoke to him:
JOSEPH	'Lodging, I beg you, good man, In the name of Heaven! My wife is weary; She says she can go no farther. Long have we travelled,

Have mercy on us good man!
God will reward you
If you will give shelter to her!'

LANDLORD   'There is no room in this place
For any stranger.
I do not know you;
Be gone, and all talking cease!
I do not care
If great distance you have come.
All of your pleading is vain
So go away, let us have our peace.'
(But then the landlord notices Mary. At once he realises he must do something to help. Pointing to one of the stables he tells Joseph that he and Mary can spend the night there. During the night Jesus is born.)

CAROL   'Away in a Manager.'

NARRATOR   'We have seen so far how these events of nearly two thousand years ago were full of surprises. Mary and Joseph had never expected to be in Bethlehem for the birth of their child – and they had certainly not expected him to be born in a stable. However the surprises were far from over, as another group of people soon found out.'

DRAMA   A group of shepherds. An angel appears at appropriate time in action.

FIRST SHEPHERD   'Going to be another cold night.'

SECOND SHEPHERD   'Too true. What shall we do to pass the time?'

FIRST SHEPHERD   'Let's have a game.'

THIRD SHEPHERD   'What of?'

FIRST SHEPHERD   'Five stones – you know – you put five stones on the ground, and pick one up and throw it in the air. While it is in the air you pick another up. You go on until you've got all the five stones in your hand at once.'

SECOND SHEPHERD   'Sounds easy.'

FIRST SHEPHERD   'Wait until you try it before you say that.'

THIRD SHEPHERD 'It's too dark to see properly anyway.'

SECOND SHEPHERD   'We've got the fire, throw a bit more wood on.'

FIRST SHEPHERD 'OK, here we go. I'll try and show you how it's done.'
(the shepherds gather round the game of five stones)

SECOND SHEPHERD   'It's funny you know, but I could have sworn it's getting lighter.'

THIRD SHEPHERD 'How could it be, it's still the middle of the night.'

FIRST SHEPHERD 'It's queer though, I thought it was getting lighter too. It's . . . aaaaaah . . . help!'
(The shepherds all shout in fear and alarm and cower down, hiding their heads. Angel appears)

ANGEL   'Lift your heads and do not be afraid.'

FIRST SHEPHERD 'That's easy to say, but that light – it's terrifying. Who are you?'

ANGEL   'I'm a messenger and I've brought you some wonderful news.'

SECOND SHEPHERD   'Wonderful news? For us? What could that be?'

ANGEL   'You are to be the first people to see a new king who has just been born.'

THIRD SHEPHERD 'Us? Poor humble shepherds like us? Why is that? Who is this new king anyway?'

ANGEL   'He is the Son of God and his name is Jesus. You will find him in a stable belonging to the inn beside the city wall.'

FIRST SHEPHERD 'All right . . . aaaaaah . . . the light again! I can't see.'
(Shepherds all cower and cover faces again. Angel disappears)

SECOND SHEPHERD   'It's all right. The light's gone out.'

THIRD SHEPHERD 'And he's gone too.'

FIRST SHEPHERD 'Do you think what he said is true?'

SECOND SHEPHERD   'I don't know, but there is only one way to find out.'

THIRD SHEPHERD 'Let's go.'

FIRST SHEPHERD 'Just a minute, just a minute. If this new baby really is a king and the Son of God I think we'd better take him a gift don't you?'

SECOND
SHEPHERD
'But what can we give him?'

THIRD SHEPHERD 'How about a lamb?'

FIRST SHEPHERD 'What a good idea. I'll get one on our way. Come on.' *(exit shepherds)*

CAROL 'While shepherds watched their flocks'

NARRATOR 'Far from Bethlehem, in the Far Eastern countries of the world, three other men got a surprise. They were not like the humble shepherds. They were rich and powerful kings. They were also very wise men. When they got over their surprise at seeing a brilliant new star in the sky, they knew that they had to follow it because it could lead them to the most important king who had ever been born. The three kings had a great distance to travel and it was many days before they reached Bethlehem.'

DRAMA The three kings – travelling.

MELCHIOR 'I think the star is stopping.'

BALTHAZAR 'After all this time.'

CASPAR 'This king must have a wonderful palace. Only the best would be good enough for the Son of God.'

MELCHIOR 'The star has stopped – but it doesn't look as if it's over a palace.'

BALTHAZAR 'That looks a very poor place indeed.'

CASPAR 'We couldn't be wrong, could we?'

MELCHIOR 'No I'm sure we couldn't. That star has led us all these miles. This must be the right place.'

BALTHAZAR 'In that case let's do this properly. Have you got the presents?'

CASPAR 'Yes – the gold and frankincense and myrrh.'

BALTHAZAR 'Very well. We'll go in with the presents, give them to the king, and then kneel to show that we worship him.'

MELCHIOR	'I agree.'
CASPAR	*(Kings 'march' round acting area and then exit to unseen area where their presentation is made. This march could be accompanied by individual/group/unison singing of 'We three kings', or by some appropriate martial music. Two appropriate pieces are 'Alla Marcia' from the Karelia Suite (Sibelius); March 'Crown Imperial' (Walton).*
NARRATOR	'A boy was born in Bethlehem With not a penny to his name, A stable bed was all he had But famous men to see him came.'

'We have seen how that first Christmas was full of surprises. Charles Dickens once said that he wished all mornings were like Christmas morning. He said this because he thought people behaved surprisingly well to each other at Christmas – often very differently to the way they behaved at other times of the year.

Bow your heads and let us listen to this prayer:

"Let us think about the service we have seen and listened to this morning. Let us remember it and try to keep the message of Christmas in our minds for all the year. Let us try to behave towards other people as we would always like them to behave to us."'

FINAL CAROL	'O Come all ye Faithful' *(all actors return to the presentation area and join in)*

Notes and sources

Carols

'Little donkey' – the percussion arrangement for this is in *Carol Gaily Carol* (see below)

'Lodging I beg you good man' – these are the words of a traditional Mexican carol

'A boy was born in Bethlehem' – from a carol by Janet Atkins, from *Faith, Folk and Festivity* (Galliard)

Additional sources

The framework of the service which has just been described provides plenty of opportunity for teachers to include original material. This is particularly so with regard to extra or alternative musical items which might be performed by either small groups, a choir, or various instrumentalists. The sources which follow offer suggestions of material from which small group musical performances might be taken.

Carol Gaily Carol, chosen by Beatrice Harrop, (A. and C. Black). Although it is now over ten years since this book first appeared it remains a very valuable source. The contents are arranged thoughtfully: Mary and the angel; The journey to Bethlehem; Seeking a place to stay; Round the crib; Shepherds and Kings; Celebrating Christmas. The accompaniments included (percussion, guitars, recorders, chime bars as well as piano) are easy and effective.

A Children's Christmas Festival by Anne Mendoza, (Oxford University Press). This is a selection for voices, recorders, tuned percussion.

The School Recorder Book of Carols by Lesley Winters, (Arnold-Wheaton). Thirteen carols, set in recorder parts, with an optional piano accompaniment.

For those schools which are looking for a more original Christmas presentation which includes words, music and instrumentalists, then the following might prove useful. All can be got on approval from:

Capital Music Centre, 64 Dean Street, London W1V 5HG (01 437 7382).

The Bell that Cried by Peter Canwell is for very young children, with a choir performing off stage.

How the Star was chosen by Barrie Turner is for infants and lower juniors and lasts about 20 minutes.

Baboushka by Charles Moreton is based on the traditional Russian tale and offers scope for a very comprehensive junior production.

The Christmas Dove and the Woodcutter is a musical play for top juniors/middle/lower secondary and has plenty of characters in it.

Holy Boy by David Palmer is over an hour long and much more sophisticated. A full-length BBC broadcast has been made of it.

Another source for 'Christmas Specials' is

Colby Music, 26a Bedford Avenue, Barnet, Herts. EN5 2EP.

Two of their recommended pieces are: *Night before Christmas* which is Clement Clarke Moore's famous poem expanded into a Christmas operetta suited to top infants and middle juniors; *Nativity according to the Animals* – singing, mime and dance for infants and juniors.

Chapter 4

Christmas dramas

Apart from major productions there is an obvious case for the smaller type of play at this time of the year. A play could be performed by a few children within a classroom; it could be performed by one class for another; it could be expanded if required to provide variety in a two-play presentation to a wider audience.

This chapter offers three suggestions for use in any of these contexts. The first suggestion is a Christmas 'Who-dun-it?' In a contemporary Christmas setting, this is a mystery in which the solution is not directly revealed to the audience – they have to solve it by spotting the clue. Such a production paves the way for an interesting discussion afterwards. The second suggestion is much less detailed and offers an opportunity for children to use their imagination to build on a simple 'starter.' The third suggestion is based on the description of an incident and the invitation to re-enact it in slow motion.

1 The Antique Shop Robbery – A Christmas 'Who-dun-it?'

Characters

Eric Dobson, owner of the antique shop
Mrs Forbes-Smyth, rather haughty, old, grey-haired and deaf
Albert Perkins, middle-aged, very scruffy, rather irritable
Detective Sergeant Terry Gibbs, who is also Eric Dobson's next-door neighbour
Four shoppers
The action takes place in Eric Dobson's antique shop. A very simple set

could consist of some draped desks on which a selection of 'antiques' is spread. The two antiques mentioned in the play are a 'valuable vase' and a 'pistol' but these could be substituted if not available, with appropriate alterations to the text.

SCENE 1

The scene opens in the antique shop. Eric is at the counter; shoppers mill around; Perkins can be seen with a large plastic carrier bag; Mrs Forbes-Smyth with a large handbag.

ERIC	*(looking at his watch and muttering to himself)* 'Ah, nearly 25 past 5. I'll be glad to get home and have my tea.'
SHOPPER 1	'Have you got all your Christmas presents?'
SHOPPER 2	'Just about – wouldn't want to buy anything in here though – too expensive!'
SHOPPER 1	'You're right there.' *(These two leave the shop)*
SHOPPER 3	'Come on Mary, it's nearly closing time and I want to get some Christmas crackers at Smiths.'
SHOPPER 4	'Righto . . . just a minute, isn't this vase lovely?' *(Picks up vase and shows to companion)*
SHOPPER 3	'It is, but you notice it hasn't got a price marked. I bet it costs a fortune. Come on.' *(These two leave the shop)*
ERIC	*(to himself)* 'Only the regulars left now. I'll just go and chat them up a bit and then . . .' *(Sound of telephone ringing off stage)* '. . . confound it, I wonder who that can be. Well, only one way to find out.' *(Eric leaves shop to answer phone. Whilst he is out Mrs Forbes-Smyth and Perkins browse about all over the shop. Both have their backs to the audience when Perkins gives a succession of loud sneezes – thus providing an opportunity for Mrs Forbes-Smyth to slip the vase into her handbag, **unnoticed by anybody**. Eric then comes back.)*
ERIC	'I must get rid of these two quickly now that the Robinsons are coming round to show us their Christmas catalogue. Now . . . **closing in two minutes folks.**'

MRS FORBES-SMYTH	'Oh Mr Dobson, I noticed a beautiful Victorian thimble back there. I'd love to buy it for my grand-daughter. How much is it?'
ERIC	*(loudly)* £25.
MRS FORBES-SMYTH	'Oh, only £5, that's very reasonable. Now just a minute, where's my purse . . .'
ERIC	*(loudly)* 'Not £5 – £25.'
MRS FORBES-SMYTH	'Yes, yes, £5 Mr Dobson, I heard you the first time.'
ERIC	*(louder)* **'Twenty-five pounds!'** *(Further into the shop Albert jumps at this bellow, drops an old pistol he has been holding and looks around guiltily.)*
MRS FORBES-SMYTH	'Manners Mr Dobson, please. There's no need to shout like that. £25 – hmmm, far too dear. I'll bid you good night.' *(Mrs Forbes-Smyth leaves shop)*
ERIC	'Closing time now please.' *(In a surly manner, clasping his carrier bag, Albert leaves the shop.)*
ERIC	'Thank goodness that's got rid of those two. Now – just a quick tidy up and then upstairs to wait for Betty and Jim.' *(Takes a duster and goes round dusting and humming to himself, suddenly comes to spot where the vase was.)*
ERIC	*(aghast)* 'It's gone! That Chinese vase – it's gone. It's worth £500 and it's gone. Now who . . . I remember now . . . I must get Terry.' *(At that moment shop door opens and Terry Gibbs walks in.)*
TERRY	'Evening Eric.'
ERIC	'Terry – I was just going to come round for you.'
TERRY	'Just on my way to the station – saw you weren't closed so popped in to see you and say Merry Christmas in case I miss you tomorrow.'
ERIC	'Nothing merry about it so far – something terrible has happened, just in this last ten minutes.'
TERRY	'Something terrible – what?'

ERIC	'Well, here, just where I'm standing was a £500, rare Chinese vase. It's just disappeared.'
TERRY	'Disappeared – how do you mean?'
ERIC	'I mean – stolen, pinched, nicked, swiped – removed, Terry!'
TERRY	'But who by – got any ideas?'
ERIC	'Oh yes. the thief was one of two people. You see, just before closing time I was in here with two regular customers – Mrs Forbes-Smyth and Albert Perkins. The phone rang out the back and I went to answer it. I distinctly remember seeing the vase as I went out. Then when I'd closed up I noticed it was gone. It could only be one of those two who took it.'
TERRY	'Had they anything they could have put it in?'
ERIC	'Both of them had. Mrs Forbes-Smyth had a big handbag, Perkins had a carrier.'
TERRY	'What are you going to do?'
ERIC	'Well, seeing as it is Christmas I'd like to give them a chance to own up, but I must have it back. Can you help? They both live within five minutes walk of here.'
TERRY	'OK Eric, I'm early anyway and it's all in the line of duty. Give me their addresses and I'll call on both of them now.' *(Terry takes out notebook)*
ERIC	'Mrs Forbes-Smyth lives in those new flats at the corner – number 25. Perkins lives in that ramshackle old Victorian house in Bury Street.' *(Terry writes this down)*
TERRY	'I'm on my way. I'll get them both back here.'

SCENE 2
Eric is in the shop. The door opens and Terry ushers in Mrs Forbes-Smyth and Albert Perkins.

MRS FORBES-SMYTH	'Mr Dobson I must protest! This policeman has said we must come back here for a matter of great importance. Really it is absolutely . . .'

TERRY	'Sit down madam, and you sir.' *(Both Mrs Forbes-Smyth and Perkins sit on two chairs facing the audience. Eric stands to one side of them, Terry to the other.)*
TERRY	'Before I do anything else, Mr Dobson has got something to say.'
ERIC	'I've just had a £500 Chinese vase stolen from the shop.'
MRS FORBES-SMYTH	'Pardon.'
ERIC	*(loudly)* 'I've just had a £500 Chinese vase stolen from the shop.'
ALBERT	'And I suppose you think I pinched it.'
TERRY	'We've got to ask some questions Mr Perkins. Do you know anything about it?'
ALBERT	'No.'
TERRY	'Did you notice it in the shop tonight?'
ALBERT	'Yes.'
TERRY	'Is it true you collect old vases?'
ALBERT	'Yes.'
TERRY	'Is it true that you've got some bills you can't pay at the moment?'
ALBERT	'What? No . . . well . . . how do you know that anyway?'
TERRY	'Is it true?'
ALBERT	'Well, I've had a bit of bad luck . . . had to sell some of my collection . . . but I never took that vase, and that's the truth!' *(Terry turns to Mrs Forbes-Smyth and speaks loudly)*
TERRY	'What do you know about the missing vase madam?'
MRS FORBES-SMYTH	'How dare you, young man!'
TERRY	*(loudly)* 'We must have your co-operation madam. Mr Dobson knows that only you and Mr Perkins were in the shop when the vase was stolen. Can you help us?'

MRS FORBES-SMYTH	'I think it's . . . just a minute . . . I think I can. I remember quite clearly now. I was at one end of the shop and Mr Perkins was at the other. I heard him give a soft sort of gasp and then I heard him whisper to himself, 'This will do.' I noticed he was holding the vase when he said this.'
ALBERT	*(leaps up in agitation)* '**What** – that's absolute rubbish!'
TERRY	'Sit down Mr Perkins please. Mr Dobson, I'm sure I now know who took the vase . . . *(At this point all of the cast look at the audience and say together:* **DO YOU?***)*

Solution

Mrs Forbes-Smyth took the vase. Mr Dobson has already said, and shown, that she was very deaf – yet she claims to have heard Mr Perkins whisper when he was at the other end of the shop. This is an obvious lie – seeking to set the blame on him.

Discussion

1 Consider the 'formula' for writing a play such as this.
   a) There are only two suspects.
   b) Both have an equal opportunity for the theft.
   c) We know at least one very important fact about one of the suspects.
   d) The culprit is caught because of telling a deliberate lie.
   After some discussion about these points the children could be invited to work out another play. The following 'facts' could be used to start things off:

> Shopping for Christmas . . . the jewellery shop . . . owner Ivor Fortune . . . Detective Sergeant Court . . . Olive Naseby, very smart and talkative . . . Ben Down, usually just in the shop to 'set his watch', lonely, likes a chat, is *left*-handed.

2 The whole moral aspect of stealing is relevant at this time of the year when shop-lifting is at its height. Some further points might be raised in this connection. (See also activity on fingerprints, p. 64.)

2   Animated waxworks

This is a dramatic activity which could either be restricted to a class exercise, or be extended to something bigger. It could be initiated by looking at a selection of old Christmas cards; the reading of some Christmas poems or stories (some of the material in Chapter 2 could be used here). Once this varied selection of Christmas themes and scenes has been discussed the children could be divided up into groups. Each group could be asked to work on the following idea.

Once the preparatory work has been done the first group forms a 'waxwork display', that is they stand motionless in a scene which depicts some aspect of Christmas, for example, carol singers, mummers, Christmas morning at home, the Wise Men. This pose is maintained for a minute or so, and then relaxed. The watching children are then asked one of two questions, either 'What happened just before the scene shown?' or 'What happened next?'

Once the answer and suggestions have been heard the waxwork group performs again. Their preparatory work will have included some dramatic activity – which starts with, or concludes with, the waxwork posed scene. The group acts out whatever scene they have prepared and a further discussion takes place to compare the watchers' original ideas with the actors' prepared interpretation.

3   The slow-motion play

This idea is based on the following description of an incident. Obviously the story is intended to be eventful, dramatic and amusing. The mime/drama which it inspires could be based on a re-creation of the incident, or a development of it into a 'What happened next?' activity. The whole mime/drama however should be done in slow motion. This is in direct contrast to the frenzy and panic engendered in the written description, and gives the opportunity for some interesting dramatic observations.

Go, George, Go!

At Christmas Miss Popney liked her infants to bring things to school. First she would say, 'Show us what you've brought', and then she would follow this up by saying, 'Now – tell us all about it.'

The day Oscar brought his dog was never to be forgotten. Oscar's dog was called George and everybody at home went about saying: 'George – that dog is mad, absolutely **M-A-D**.' He was a large, friendly-looking mongrel.

When Oscar brought him to school everything seemed peaceful at first. George let the other children stroke him and Miss Popney, who was very nervous of dogs, sighed with relief. That is until George quietly fastened his teeth into Oliver Kmetz's trousers and with a quick jerk of his head tore them clean into two pieces.

Oliver let out a yell, clasping his hands over his white and suddenly exposed bottom; several of the girls screamed. Nobody heard Oscar whisper, 'Go, George, go!'

George bounded up the aisle and leapt onto Miss Popney's desk. With a friendly gesture he pushed his face close to the teacher's, one half of the Kmetz trousers still dangling from his jaws.

'Oscar!' screamed Miss Popney, flinging her arms wide and sending pencils, books and a Bavarian cuckoo clock hurtling to the floor. The clock hit the floor with a splintering crash and the bird got half way through its opening hatch to mutter a strangled 'Cuck . . .', before being jerked backwards as if by an invisible hand. There was an immediate shriek from Michelle Gwyn – she had brought the cuckoo clock to show and talk about.

Oscar smiled – he reckoned Miss Popney would not ask him to say much about George.

Chapter 5

Christmas today

The concern of this chapter is with contemporary events. There are comments on the modern Santa Claus; work for children which is related to crime at this time of the year; facts about deserving causes who might be helped; some reflections by people for whom Christmas is a particularly busy time of the year.

Helping others

Christmas is, of course, an ideal time to do something to help people less fortunate than ourselves. At the same time there are many charitable organisations who could make a claim for money raised at organised carol singing outings, Christmas concerts, or via special campaigns linked to some aspect of the festival. How then does one choose to whom money should be given?

The comments contained here obviously do not seek to portray one charity as being more deserving than others, but they do seek to highlight some charities which have a particular relevance to children.

1   Action Research for the Crippled Child.

This organisation adopted the Paddington Bear character and formed Paddington's Action Club. An annual subscription of £3.50 (1984) brings contributors a Paddington badge, a membership card, a birthday card, an annual magazine and three newsletters.

Details from: Paddington's Action Club
              Vincent House, North Parade,
              Horsham, West Sussex RH12 2DA

2   Save the Children Fund

This is another organisation which invites children to help a worthy cause whilst at the same time offering them the opportunity to join a club. There are three ways in which they can become club members:

a) by joining as an individual
b) by joining with friends as a youth or club organisation
c) by joining through school when the latter is a school league member.

Attractions include a badge for individual members, pennants for groups, membership cards and copies of the magazine 'Satellite.'

Details from: Young Save the Children Fund
17 Grove Lane
London SE5 8RD

3   Foster Parents Plan

This is a different kind of organisational charity, which works as follows. For £9 a month a class, or school, can become a 'Foster parent' to a boy or girl in one of twenty-two countries in Africa, Asia or Latin America. This usually results in a two-way correspondence of letters, photographs, drawings, etc.

For example, a *Yorkshire Evening Post* article described in detail how a class of nine and ten year-olds in a Knaresborough primary school spent one Christmas thinking particularly of thirteen year-old Vic-Mar Manzano, a Filipino boy. Vic-Mar was 'adopted' by class 5H of Aspin Park County Primary School because, living with his mother and brothers and sisters in a tiny house made of corrugated iron sheeting, there was insufficient money for his basic needs. A Christmas sale of books and comics was one of Aspin's money-raising ideas.

Details from: National Director
Foster Parents Plan
Third Floor, 315 Oxford Street, London W1R 1LA

4   Physically Handicapped and Able Bodied

With the current educational philosophy of trying to cater for children with special needs in ordinary schools, this organisation is one to which 'giving' may be particularly significant for children. It claims that 'school age is exactly the right time for the PHAB philosophy to be introduced – the integration of physically handicapped children with those who are able bodied. If the barriers are broken down early, then for the rest of their lives it won't be a problem. Simply, it works!'

Teachers will obviously find much to agree with in this statement.
Details from: Sir Peter Baldwin, KCB,
Physically Handicapped and Able Bodied
Tavistock House North
Tavistock Square
London WC1H   9HX

5   Royal Commonwealth Society for the Blind

This is another organisation which provides the opportunity for children to
make a specific contribution to individuals, and to learn more about them.
For instance, the September 1984, newsletter detailed how two East Afri-
can children, Moja and David, received Braille kits – containing a Braille
writing frame, embossed ruler and tape measure, abacus and special board
for raised drawings. These kits had been bought with £32 raised by a Kent
junior school.
Details from: Alan Johns
Royal Commonwealth Society for the Blind
Commonwealth House
Haywards Heath
West Sussex RH16 3AZ

Many schools may, because of their own circumstances or local influence,
want to contribute to other charities at Christmas. The following address list
may therefore be of some help.
Age Concern England, Bernard Sunley House, 60 Pitcairn Road, Mitcham,
Surrey CR4 3LL
Dr Barnardo's, Tanners Lane, Ilford, Essex 1GG 1QG
British Red Cross Society, 9 Grosvenor Crescent, London SW1Y 5AR
Christain Aid, PO Box 1, London SW9 8BH
Help the Aged, 24 Wingate Trading Estate, High Road, Tottenham,
London N17 0DA
National Canine Defence League, 10 Seymour Street, London W1H 5WB
National Children's Home, Ambrose Lane, Harpenden, Herts. AL5 4BY
National Deaf Children's Society, 45 Hereford Road, London W25 5AH
NSPCC, PO Box 39, Burton on Trent, DE14 3LQ
Oxfam, Murdoch Road, Bicester, Oxon. OX6 7RF
UNICEF, 84 Broomfield Road, Chelmsford, Essex CM1 1SS
   If a school chooses to sell charity Christmas cards then the following
addresses may be useful:
Charity Christmas Cards Council, 49 Lamb's Conduit Street, London
WC1N 3N6

The 1959 Group of Charities, same address as above.
These two organisations are run independently of each other even though they are based at the same address.

The Modern Santa Claus

Perhaps the first thing to say about the modern Santa Claus is that he exists in thousands of places!

In Britain, for instance, his annual resurrection begins in February. This is when Bermans, a London theatrical costumier, starts to hire out Santa Claus costumes to photographic studios who are preparing for their November/December advertising campaigns. Nearer to the festival itself the costumes are again in great demand for bazaars and fetes.

Many large department stores employ Santa Clauses who give out presents to the children who come shopping. Harrods, the world-famous Knightsbridge store has a team who are chosen for their similarity of height so that they can take it in turns to receive the children. At Selfridges, it has been estimated that by the time he has finished his 'season' their Santa Claus will have shaken about three-quarters of a million hands.

In the United States of America the Santa Claus cult is even stronger. There is a small town in the state of Indiana called Santa Claus, and every year 3 000 000 letters arrive there addressed to Santa Claus. There is also a statue of him on Kriss Kringle Street.

Near Lake Placid in New York State is another evocatively-named small town – North Pole. In North Pole there is 'Santa's Workshop' which is a sort of Christmas Disneyland. It contains Santa's house, complete with Santa, rocking chair, lollipops and a grandfather clock which conceals a hidden camera; the Reindeer Barn from which sleigh rides can be taken; a giant Christmas tree and an assortment of craft shops selling gifts.

There is also a Santa Claus at the real North Pole, or at least near to it. Five miles north of Rovaniemi in Finnish Lapland, and on the edge of the Arctic Circle, is 'Arctic Circle Cottage.' The long, log cabin contains a souvenir shop, a cafeteria – and the room where those thousands of letters addressed to 'Santa Claus, North Pole' finally arrive.

These letters, from children as far apart as Australia and Russia, Britain and Japan, and numbering more than 40 000 annually, are dealt with by Santa Claus and his seventeen 'brownie' helpers. The letters are sorted into boxes, by country, and then answered by a standard reply from Santa Claus which is printed on an illustrated card. This card is reproduced in ten different languages and obviously goes to world-wide destinations. Arctic Circle Cottage also has ten special telephone lines so that Santa Claus can be telephoned as well. This service, however, is only available to children who live in Finland.

This letter-reply service of Santa, from Arctic Circle Cottage, costs thousands of pounds every year, and the money to support it comes from the Finnish Post Office, the national and local tourist boards, and the Ministry of Labour.

The church with 124 Father Christmases

St Botolph was a man known for his kindness to others and his monastery in Suffolk was a place where travellers and strangers always knew they would be made welcome for a meal or an overnight stay. In Aldgate, East London, there is a church named after this saint and in its crypt is a community centre which is famous throughout the district.

In London there are many people who are in need of help. Often they have no money, no friends, no homes, and are sometimes in poor health as well. St Botolph's Crypt tries to give these people both help and advice. They can go there out of the cold and have food and hot drinks. There are showers so that they can get cleaned up and medical advice is available for those who want it. Apart from these things there are talks given on a wide range of subjects, and Friday nights are 'social nights' when there are video shows, snooker, pool and other games to play.

It is at Christmas however when people without homes are most desperate, and this is when those who work at St Botolph's Crypt make a special effort. In 1983, on December 22, seventy-two people were given a sit-down lunch and entertained by a group of musicians playing Christmas music. In the church itself a free concert was given by a member of the Guildhall School of Music, and various visitors to the crypt were taken to live theatre performances in London. Christmas Day was made special for ninety people who had nowhere else to go. They were given a full Christmas dinner in the crypt, even though it was a tight squeeze to get them all in.

Of course it is not possible to do things like this without either people to help or money to buy the food. St Botolph's Crypt has a number of people who work there permanently either full- or part-time, but during 1984 one hundred and twenty four volunteers regularly helped out. The church organises events, like the Christmas Fayre advertised in the leaflet, to raise money to run the centre.

The work being done at St Botolph's Crypt should help to remind us that Jesus said, when we welcomed the hungry and those who were strangers, we welcomed Him. (Ref: Matthew 25, vs. 31–46)

We would gratefully receive all your oddments of bright-coloured wools

and scraps of materials for use in our craft classes!

St. Botolph's Day Centre   Aldgate. London EC3N 1AB   Telephone 01-283 1950/1670

Day Centre Co-ordinator:
Daly Maxwell

Our ref
Your ref
Date NOVEMBER 1984

S O S

CHRISTMAS FAYRE 1984

DEAR FRIENDS

EVERY YEAR AT CHRISTMAS TIME WE MAKE A SPECIAL
EFFORT TO RAISE BADLY NEEDED FUNDS. GIFTS FOR THE
STALLS AT OUR CHRISTMAS FAYRE WOULD BE GRATEFULLY
RECEIVED. ANY UNWANTED OR SURPLUS ITEMS WOULD BE
A GREAT HELP TO US.

WE NEED FOR THE STALLS

GIFT ITEMS - TOILETRIES, ETC.

BOOKS - ESPECIALLY PAPER BACKS.

TOYS & GAMES - IN GOOD CONDITION.

BRIC-A-BRAC - AND OTHER ODDS AND

ENDS OF ALL KINDS.

GROCERIES - JARS, PACKETS,

TINS, ETC., AND

HOME PRODUCE.

IF ALL OUR PARISHIONERS, LOCAL RESIDENTS, BUSINESS
MEN AND WOMEN, SHOPKEEPERS AND STREET TRADERS MADE
A CONTRIBUTION, HOWEVER SMALL, FOR THE STALLS, WE
WOULD HAVE A BUMPER CHRISTMAS FAYRE ON DECEMBER 5TH,
TO BE HELD IN THE CHURCH BETWEEN 11.00AM AND 3.00PM.

GIFTS MAY BE HANDED IN AT THE CHURCH. PETTICOAT SQUARE AND TOWER
RESIDENTS MAY DELIVER CONTRIBUTIONS TO 604 PETTICOAT SQUARE,
OR RING 247-6714, 283-1950, OR 283-1670 TO ARRANGE FOR COLLECTION.
ONE OF THE ST BOTOLPH'S STAFF OR A VOLUNTEER WORKER WILL VISIT
SHOPKEEPERS AND TRADERS DURING THE WEEK OF NOVEMBER 26TH TO 30TH
TO COLLECT ANY GIFTS OR DONATIONS FOR THE FAYRE.

PLEASE HELP US TO HELP OTHERS

WE THANK YOU ALL IN ADVANCE.

THE STAFF AND VOLUNTEERS OF ST BOTOLPH'S CRYPT CENTRE.
Rector: The Revd Malcolm Johnson

Crime at Christmas

One of the sad facts about Christmas today is that it is a peak time of the year for shop-lifting and petty thieving.

A classroom discussion about this type of crime could be held to find out why the children think people steal – is it for a 'dare'? Is it because they are poor, unemployed or bored? The discussion could lead on to further talk about police efforts to combat such crime. In connection with the latter the children would probably enjoy doing some work to prove the truth of the statement that no two sets of fingerprints are alike.

Two very simple methods of recording fingerprints are as follows.

1 Carefully smooth out a piece of plasticine and get the children to press their fingers in it to make prints.
2 Fix a fairly long piece of sellotape in place on a desk, sticky side upwards. The children can then rub their fingers on a piece of chalk, and press the chalked finger tips onto the sticky side of the sellotape.

This topic could also provide the opportunity to invite an officer from the local station to come and talk about crime prevention.

'Today I spoke to . . .'

Children of today are all familiar with the way that information is provided via interviews. A TV news bulletin rarely passes without at least one interview.

Using this contemporary activity, and linking it with some detailed re-search and imagination, can result in some very worthwhile pre-Christmas work. One of the first ways to go about it is to discuss what any given person in Bethlehem at the time of Jesus' birth might have noticed, talked about, and thought of the events which took place. Further discussion might then centre on the most pertinent questions to ask this person so that a background picture of facts and opinions emerge.

Once this has been done it is essential to provide the children with some good reference material so that they can look up details of relevant issues. Two very useful books in this context are: *The Book of the Bible*, written by a team of authors and published by Purnell, and *The New Black's Bible Dictionary* by M.S. and J. Lane Miller and published by A. and C. Black.

Next, the series of interviewers and interviewees could prepare their material and tape 'the interviews.' The end product would then provide some unusual and interesting background comment to the traditional Christmas story. Once the interviews have been taped the possibilities for linking them with mime, drama, music, painting, become obvious.

There follows here a suggestion of 'people who might be interviewed' and a specimen example of an 'interview' which took place under the circumstances described.

Possible interviewees

a) Joseph
b) Mary
c) A fellow traveller on the way to Bethlehem
d) A peddler at the city walls
e) The innkeeper
f) A person who lives in the same street as the inn
g) A boy or girl of 11 (or whatever age is appropriate) who worked at the inn. (A useful reference here might be to the story *Sam and the Midnight Music*, p. 24)
h) One of Caspar's servants
i) An astronomer of the time
j) A Roman soldier given orders to kill the baby boys in Bethlehem

An interview with Ahijah, a resident of Bethlehem

INTERVIEWER   'Ahijah, I believe you live in Bethlehem.'

AHIJAH   'Oh yes indeed, lovely little town.'

INTERVIEWER   'Can you tell us a bit about it?'

AHIJAH   'Well, it is quite small with a wall round it. The streets are very narrow and have flat-roofed houses on either side. It doesn't take many people to make it look crowded. It's quite a hilly place and towards the south a valley drops all the way down to the Dead Sea.'

INTERVIEWER   'What is your own home like?'

AHIJAH   'Outside we've got a courtyard where the cooking and baking goes on. We keep a couple of goats there too. In the summer we sleep on the flat roof, in the winter our bedroom is on the inside but on the top floor. We use rush mats for eating off and for sitting and sleeping on. Downstairs the house always seems a bit dark because the windows are small and high. We use a lamp down there. It is made of clay and burns olive oil.'

INTERVIEWER   'What is your job?'

AHIJAH   'Oh, I'm a carpenter like that Joseph fellow. Out at dawn I am with just a handful of bread and a few olives. A bit of goat cheese with raisins and bread for dinner and then home at night.'

INTERVIEWER   'You mention Joseph. Were you at Bethlehem when Jesus was born?'

AHIJAH   'I'll say I was. Never seen anything like it – ever!'

INTERVIEWER   'Can you tell us a bit about it?'

AHIJAH   'If my memory serves me right, and I'm sure it does, it all started with the census. People pouring in from everywhere under the sun to be enrolled; extra Roman soldiers drafted in to keep order; pandemonium everywhere.'

INTERVIEWER   'Did you actually see Joseph and Mary?'

AHIJAH   'No, never set eyes on them, but I remember that night their son was born.'

INTERVIEWER   'Why is that?'

AHIJAH   'A friend of mine lived near the city wall and I was visiting him. "See those caves," he said, pointing up to the hillsides where a thousand lights flickered. "Should be animals in them but they're full of people. Same in town here. They've had to move animals over to get the people in." Anyway there we were, playing draughts, and sipping a little wine when there was this commotion.'   .

INTERVIEWER   'What was that?'

AHIJAH   'Shepherds would you believe – on a city street. Looked a mess they did with their long hair and beards – even a bit frightening with their abas over their heads.'

INTERVIEWER   'Abas – what are they?'

AHIJAH   'A sort of huge cloak they pull over their heads in storms and cold weather. Almost like walking tents they were really. And as they walked the bags full of pebbles they kept for throwing to attract the sheeps' attention were rattling all the time.'

INTERVIEWER   'Where did they go?'

AHIJAH   'Straight to the cave which belonged to an inn in the street. Even had a lamb with them they did.'

INTERVIEWER   'Did they say anything?'

AHIJAH   'Not then – but our game of draughts went on a long time and when it was almost dawn they came out of the cave

	place, shouting and cheering. We called out to them: 'What is it? What's been going on?'
INTERVIEWER	'What did they say?'
AHIJAH	'Shouted back, "We've seen a king who has just been born – great news – he's going to save us all. Tell your friends the fantastic news!"'
INTERVIEWER	'Did you?'
AHIJAH	'Oh yes. I've never seen ordinary people so excited. They convinced you that something marvellous had happened. It was odd really – the way those ordinary fellows managed to do that. I really felt I'd been given some terrific news – and I was keen to pass it on.'
INTERVIEWER	'So you actually saw something of what happened on that special night?'
AHIJAH	'I did indeed, but if you want to know more about what happened at the inn why don't you talk to . . .'

How does Christmas affect you?

Schools are communities where children and teachers enjoy a fairly predictable range of community activities, which obviously end when the term is finished and everybody disperses to their own homes.

For people in other walks of life however, pre-Christmas activities, and sometimes Christmas itself, is very different. For some it is a particularly busy time of the year, for others it is 'business as usual,' for others again it is either frustrating in some way or particularly satisfying.

To get their reactions to this time of the year I spoke to a range of people who included a nurse, a farmer's daughter, a parish priest and a professional entertainer. The public relations officer of a supermarket chain and a postmaster gave me some behind-the-scenes information about their fields, and the biography of an ex-jockey provided an insight into a very 'different' Christmas.

In the shops

One of the members of Tesco's Public Affairs Department told me that Christmas was probably the busiest time of the year for people who work in supermarkets. At Tesco Christmas really begins in September. This is the time when the stores start to 'project' their Christmas material and the stores' buyers start to plan what range of toys and other goods will gradually become apparent in the stores as the season draws nearer.

For the people who actually work in the supermarkets Christmas means a time when they work overtime to cope with the rush, and temporary staff are employed to help at this busy time. Every store also arranges its own celebrations for the staff and a Christmas dinner is provided for all.

Sportsmen

Another group of people for whom the Christmas period is a busy one are jockeys. On Boxing Day there are many important horse races in various parts of the country. The jockeys who ride the horses in these races have to keep their weight down, because the less weight a horse carries the more likely it is to win.

Terry Biddlecombe, who was a famous champion jockey, has said that Christmas for him was a strange time of the year. Whilst the rest of his family were enjoying their Christmas dinner, and his mother was trying to persuade him to have some, he went down to the cellar of his house. There he climbed into a box which was heated by lots of 150-watt light bulbs. Seated in a deck chair with his sweat suit on he thought of all the lovely food being eaten upstairs whilst he had only an occasional drink.

In hospitals

For hospital staff, work goes on regardless of the fact that most people are on holiday at this time of the year. Sue, a trainee nurse at a busy hospital on the outskirts of London, told me what it was like in a hospital ward on Christmas Day.

'It's a day when everybody makes a really special effort. Obviously most of the patients would rather be at home with their families and friends but, despite this, they all seem to try to be extra specially cheerful on this day in particular. As for us nurses, well we become two people in one. First of all we have to do our work and provide the patients with the care they need, but we also try to cheer them up, and sometimes off-duty nurses give up their own time to 'dress up' and go and entertain some of the more lonely patients. I have worked on both children's and old people's wards on Christmas day and can honestly say there isn't another day quite like it in the whole year. I always felt pleased that I lived near to the hospital though – so I could spend some time with my own family!'

Entertainers

Dennis Patten is a conjuror and magician who gives many live performances and has appeared on TV and in films. Perhaps the best known film he has been in is 'Chitty-Chitty Bang Bang.'

Christmas for him is a very busy time and one of the things he does is give shows for schools. This sees him dashing about from school to school entertaining large numbers of children with conjuring tricks. He tries to make every show he does as perfect as possible and, as he told me he is still nervous before he performs, this is an enjoyable but tiring part of his work.

Perhaps the best way to appreciate how good Dennis Patten is, is not to watch him when he performs, but to watch faces of the children in his audience.

On the farm

Sally Furness lives on a farm at Baslow, near Bakewell in Derbyshire. She told me that the main difference between Christmas day and any other day is simply that it starts earlier – but like all days on the farm, it is very busy!

'My father gets up and goes out at 5.30am', she said. 'He is joined by his two helpers and they set to work milking the 85-strong milking herd of cows. This takes place two hours before the customary milking time because the tanker comes earlier as it is Christmas day and the driver wants to finish work as early as possible. The cows are milked again at 4pm.

While the morning milking is taking place another helper feeds the rest of the animals so they eat earlier than usual. The bullocks, hens and sheep are not given any special treats but the old horse, Meg, usually gets some extra oats. The morning session finishes about 9.30am, work begins again at 4pm and finishes for the day at about 6pm.

For the workers, although the day is not a holiday, some effort is made to make it a little special. Morning coffee is supplemented with a more seasonal drink, there are mince pies as well as sandwiches and wage packets are a 'little heavier.'

Christmas dinner for the family is in the traditional style although the turkey may be replaced with a freshly-killed chicken from the farm. So whilst Christmas day is never a holiday for the farmer, some changes in the times when things are done, allow him and his helpers to spend more time with their families.

At the Post Office

Vic Winfield is the Head Postmaster at the busy Enfield, North London sorting office. He described how the work load at the Post Office increases enormously in the pre-Christmas period.

'We always advertise the latest recommended posting dates so that letters will reach their destination by Christmas. In 1984 these dates were 17 December for first class mail and parcels, and 19 for second class mail. We also try our best to deliver as much mail as we can which is posted after these dates.

The level of postings gradually increases during the first week of any December but many of our customers traditionally prepare their Christmas cards over the last but one weekend before Christmas, resulting in peak postings on the following Monday. It can be seen from this that the day of the week on which Christmas falls is important for the Post Office.

The fact that Tuesday was Christmas Day in 1984 meant that this was one of the worst days for the Post Office. Many people do respond to advice to post early however and Monday, 17 December, was 1984's peak day. One hundred million items (two and a half times the normal workload) were posted throughout the country on this date.

At the Enfield sorting office special arrangements for Christmas began on 10 December. By this time the processing of 350 000 to 450 000 posted letters and packets per day had started; this again was two and a half times the normal rate. To help with deliveries the work force was increased by about a third. This meant about 130 extra people (students, wives, unemployed, retired people, etc.) were employed.

There are more complications. The huge increase in letters and parcels means that more transport is needed. At Enfield we hired an extra thirty-one vans for Christmas 1984. This was an increase of fifty per cent over our normal transport fleet and in itself caused more problems. Because extra sorting office space was necessary a garage/car parking area had to be used for this and therefore extra van parking space had to be hired in a cinema car park.

Because of the increase in mail, deliveries take much longer. The first delivery takes all morning and the second delivery is not completed until late afternoon. As well as the usual deliveries on Christmas Eve, there is also one on the Sunday before Christmas day, 23 December in 1984.

One of the saddest things about Christmas at the Post Office is finding that so many cards in particular are inadequately addressed. Most of these cards do not have return addresses and the main reason for them not reaching their destination is because the envelopes carry 'half-remembered addresses' or ones written illegibly by children. The Post Office does its best in these circumstances and all undeliverable items (including those damaged through poor packaging) are kept for some time in the hope that they might be claimed later. The Post Office has a name for where all these items are kept – 'Heartbreak Corner.'

The main disadvantage of working for the Post Office at Christmas is that all the extra time involved means less time available to spend with one's family. There are advantages however and it is both stimulating and rewarding when advance plans work out well. For me personally one of the pleasantest things is meeting people like MPs and Mayors who like to see the Post Office at work during its busiest time. Visits by such people are very good for morale.'

In churches

Canon Robin Osborne is the vicar of St Mary's with St Paul's parish church in Penzance, Cornwall. He told me something about the organisation and pleasure in the link between Christmas preparations and the church.

Schools, for instance, tend to prepare a long way ahead and some reserve time in church as much as twelve months ahead. Canon Osborne also commented on how school services have changed over the years, with the traditional nine carols and lessons services often now being replaced with services which include more action, drama, and use of varied musical instruments. Apart from schools, colleges and choral societies also reserve the church for special services at Christmas time. Whilst the choice of congregational music hardly varies and the same printed order of service lasts from year to year, the church choir supplies the 'icing on the cake' at Christmas, and often begins its preparations in October.

I asked Canon Osborne about the actual number of people who came to church at Christmas and he said that the number of communicants who attend the midnight service is double that of a normal Sunday communion service, and the actual number of people present is treble the normal. With regard to the extra work in which he is involved he said that this depended to some extent to which day Christmas fell. Sometimes it was possible to have almost forty-eight hours of non-stop services and with visiting hospitals and the like the Vicar was in almost constant demand, supplementing his usual duties by being 'the link man, verger, chap who knows where the switches are and one who "says a few words."'

When asked what were the pleasures of being a parish priest at Christmas, Canon Osborne said how much he appreciated the openness of people at this time of the year; the satisfaction of being able to supply something which people want in the way of a 'plant'; and the opportunity of being able to proclaim the Gospel at a time when people respond so well to the sense of occasion and celebration.

Chapter 6 🌿

Christmas and other cultures

Christmas is a festival of celebration. It can also be the starting point for an examination of the festivals of celebration of other religions and cultures, many of which are practised in Britain today. Some of these events, such as *Chanukkah* and *Dipavali*, take place at about the same time as Christmas. Others are at different times of the year but share the theme of celebration.

The timing of festivals

Before giving details of particular festivals it is necessary to make some comment about their calendar location. The timing of festivals of different faiths is governed by various calendars and this makes any sort of perennial arrangement so complex as to be virtually impossible. For instance the Gregorian Calendar, which is solar-based and used in most Western countries, enables most festivals related to it to be fixed. An exception is Easter which is a moveable feast. The Jewish calendar is lunar-based and to adjust it to the solar year an extra (embolismic) month is added seven times in each nineteen-year period. The Islamic calendar is lunar-based without adjustment and this means that Muslim festivals advance by about eleven or twelve days each year. More than one calendar is in use in India.

Thus for the teacher or child who wants to know 'When exactly is it?' the question may often only be answered by reference to the current year. As an excellent annual guide to these matters I strongly recommend *The Calendar of Religious Festivals* which is published by The Commission for Racial Equality, Elliott House, 10–12 Allington Street, London SW1E 5EH.

Festivals which can be related to Christmas

If we think of Christmas in the context of a 'birth' theme then other festivals which can be related to it include *Wesak* (Buddhist), *Janam Ashtami* (Hindu), *Meelad-ul-Nabi* (Muslim) and *Guru Nanak* (Sikh).

Chanukkah (Jewish) and *Dipavali* (Hindu) relate well to Christmas within a 'light/darkness' theme, and *Hijrah* (Muslim) is a festival which could be joined with Christmas in celebrating a 'beginning.'

Details of these festivals follow and links with Christmas can be made as and when teachers feel they are suitable.

Wesak

Wesak is a Buddhist festival which celebrates three things:
1 the birth of Siddartha Gautama, who became the Buddha
2 his 'enlightenment', thirty-five years later
3 his death, at the age of eighty.

According to the Therevada tradition, these three important dates in the life of the Buddha all fell on the full-moon day in the month of *Vesakha* (April/May in the Gregorian calendar). *Wesak* is therefore a three-day festival.

During the celebrations for *Wesak* houses are decorated with lanterns and there are great processions. Presents are exchanged and gifts are made to the poor. Captive birds are freed in memory of the Buddha's kindness. Candles are lit and people gather together to meditate before images of the Buddha.

Some useful words in connection with this festival are:
Buddharupa – a small shrine which holds an image of the Buddha;
Stupa – the name given to a place of prayer;
Dhamma – the law or teaching of Buddha;
Sangha – the name given to the order of monks which was founded by the Buddha.

Janam Ashtami

Janam Ashtami is a Hindu festival which celebrates the birth of Lord Krishna. Krishna was born from a black hair which Vishnu, the great God and Creator, plucked from his own head. The anniversary falls in the western months of either August or September. The festival is celebrated at midnight – the time when Lord Krishna was born.

Worshippers spend the day before the festival fasting and praying, and the temples in which they worship often have an image of Lord Krishna as a baby in a cradle. After the day of fasting there are celebrations with singing and plays about Krishna's life. Special sweets are put in Krishna's cradle.

The teachings of Lord Krishna are contained in a book called *Bhagavad Gita*, which means 'Song of the Blessed Lord.' Here is a verse from it:

'He who offers to me with devotion only a leaf, or a flower, or a fruit, or even a little water, this I accept from that yearning soul, because with a pure heart it was offered with love.' 9:26

Meelad-ul-Nabi

Meelad-ul-Nabi is the Muslim festival which celebrates the birthday of Muhammad. Muslims consider Muhammad the most important person who ever lived and whenever his name is spoken the words 'peace be on him' are then said.

Muhammad was born on 12 *Rabi-ul-Awal* in the Muslim calendar (20 August, AD 570). Not only is the day of his birth commemorated but the whole month is considered special. The 'Prophet's Day' is celebrated with stories of the birth and life of Muhammad. There are ceremonial readings, supported by prayers and thoughts about the words of the Prophet.

The *Qur'an* is the Holy Book containing the message which God told Muhammad to spread. Muhammad said that every Muslim must base his life on the 'Five Pillars of Wisdom', these are:

1 The belief in only one God (*Shahada*)
2 Prayer five times a day (*Salat*)
3 Giving to the poor (*Zakat*)
4 Fasting for thirty days during the month of *Ramadan* (*Saum*)
5 Making at least one pilgrimage to Mecca (*Hajj*).

Guru Nanak

This festival celebrates the birth of Guru Nanak, the founder of the Sikh religion. Its calender location is variable because of the Indian *Bikrami* calendar.

On the day before the commemoration itself a great procession is held. Music and crowds accompany a float carrying the canopied platform which contains the Sikh Holy Book. On the day which celebrates Guru Nanak's birth there is a long period of worship (*Diwau*) which leads up to the time he was actually born. After this there are readings from the Holy Book and then meals are served to all in a 'free kitchen.'

Guru Nanak gave the basic teaching of Sikhism in the Mul Mantra:

> 'There is One God. His name is Eternal Truth. He is the maker of all things and He lives in all things. He is without fear and without enmity. His image is timeless.'

Chanukkah (Hanukkah)

Chanukkah is the Jewish Festival of Light which reminds worshippers of events which took place over two thousand years ago. At that time the Syrians conquered the Jews, banned all the Jewish holy days and destroyed religious things. The Jews fought back and with Judas Maccabee as their leader they defeated the Syrians. The people then set about repairing the

Temple. When the Jews re-lit the Temple lamp there was only a small quantity of oil in it. Miraculously this tiny amount of oil kept the lamp lit for eight days. In remembrance of this the *Chanukkah* festival lasts for eight days.

The festival takes place during the Jewish months of *Kislev* and *Tevet* and occurs just before the Christian Christmas. The celebrations centre round the *menorah* – a nine-branched candlestick. On the first evening of the festival one candle is lit and put in the menorah, on the second evening another is lit, and so on until all the candles are alight. The ninth place on the candlestick is for the candle from which all the others have been lit.

As *Chanukkah* is one of the happiest of festivals there is much present giving and eating of special food like *latkes* (potato pancakes). A very popular spinning game is often played in homes. This game uses a *dreidel*, which is a four-sided top. The markings on each of the sides are illustrated in Figure 1.

shin	hay	gimmel	nun
=put in	=take half	=get all	=get nothing

Figure 1

Some sweets or coins are put in the centre of the table. The first player spins the dreidel and acts according to how it lands. For instance, if *gimmel* lands uppermost that player gets all the sweets or money. These Jewish dreidel markings include the Hebrew initial letters of the phrase:

'Nes gadol hayah sham' ('A great miracle happened there.')

Dipavali (Diwali)

Dipavali is the Hindu Festival of Light. It celebrates 'new beginnings', the return of Rama after his triumph over Ravana, the triumph of good over evil. It is a five-day festival, the third day being *Dipavali* proper, and it usually takes place in the Western calendar month of November.

Lights are the outstanding feature of this festival. *Deepa* (lamps) are ceremonially lit everywhere; cities are illuminated with coloured lights;

fairy lights and candles can be seen all around. Inside homes the lights are traditionally made by burning mustard oil in clay pots. One of the reasons for so many lights is that everyone wants to welcome Lakshmi – who is the goddess of prosperity and who visits homes which are brightly lit.

Before the festival starts Hindu mothers prepare large quantities of savouries and cakes. These are given to guests and are taken as gifts to family gatherings and parties. People wear new clothes whenever possible, and before putting them on they often rub their bodies with sweet-smelling oils. The eating, parties and exchange of presents take place against a background of music and dancing. The whole celebration is one of light, colour and noise – not forgetting the giving of thanks for past prosperity and prayers for the future.

The Day of Hijrah

The Day of *Hijrah* is a Muslim celebration which could be incorporated in a theme of 'beginnings.' It commemorates Muhammad's flight from Mecca to Medina.

When Muhammad was living in Mecca he tried to teach others that there was only one God. Although he convinced some people, others thought that such an idea would cause them to lose business because they made money by selling images of all the different idols. Many did not like Muhammad's teaching that duty to Allah (God) was essential. As a result a plot to kill Muhammad was organised, and the prophet had to flee to Medina in the year AD 622. Muslims now believe that this was the year in which the religion of Islam was founded.

Celebrations commemorating the Day of *Hijrah* include the sending of greetings to friends and relations, and the re-telling of the stories of Muhammad and his companions. Included amongst the stories are those detailing how the prophet returned to Mecca in AD 630 and established it as the Holy City for Muslims.

Chapter 7

Behind the scenes at a pantomime

In medieval times Christmas entertainment for ordinary people was provided by troupes of mummers. However, at Christmas balls in grand stately homes the guests were often entertained by dancers. From these beginnings the first pantomime evolved – a dramatic action which was literally all in the mime and portrayed by dancers.

From these origins pantomimes have developed considerably. Some are costly commercial ventures where the plot is often rather warped to accommodate a star performer; other productions seek to follow a more traditional pattern. In this, the main plot is usually based on a well-known story and the hero or heroine moves through a series of adventures (humorous, romantic, etc.) to ultimate success and happiness.

Whatever the production, the modern pantomime, when staged in a professional theatre is a complex commercial and artistic venture. Just how complex I found out when, mainly thanks to the good offices of Ann Mottershead and Cliff Dix, I attached myself to the production of 'Dick Whittington' at the Playhouse, Harlow, one of Britain's busiest regional theatres.

Behind the scenes
Getting the costs right

There would obviously be no pantomimes if there was not careful costing to make sure that sufficient money was brought in to sustain the show. This involves a great deal of preparatory work. For instance, at the Playhouse, Harlow, Anne Mottershead has to make sure as many people as possible know that the pantomime is actually going to take place. Publicity for it starts early and builds up as production time gets nearer.

The early publicity is given in advance brochures about forthcoming events at the theatre, and in newspaper advertisements. Twenty-two thousand brochures include early information about the show and these are gradually reinforced by 250 posters, 15 000 handbills and ultimately 2500 programmes. Advertisement sheets, printed balloons and small gifts are also included in 'give-away' publicity campaigns, and the help of local firms is enlisted. Firms are offered the opportunity to advertise in the theatre whilst the show is on. In return for this they make a contribution towards costs.

Booking for the show starts on 1 August and there is always an early rush. Block booking is encouraged and one means of doing this is to offer one free ticket in 10, to parties of over 20 who have booked seats at performances where reductions are offered. It can be seen that careful calculation is always needed with regard to seats and prices. In the Playhouse, for instance, there are 297 seats in the centre of the auditorium which are sold for the pantomime performances at £2.45 each (£2.20 when reduced), 64 seats in the side wings at the back which sell at £2.15 each (£1.95 when reduced), 74 seats in the two wings at the side and 29 seats in the balcony which sell at £1.65 (£1.40 when reduced)! No reductions are offered for Saturday performances or on Boxing Day and New Year's Day.

Performances run from mid-December to mid-January and 12 000 people are expected to see the show during its run.

The box office
When people book a seat for a pantomime three things are important:
1 The cost of the seat,
2 Where the seat is,
3 The date and time of the performance they wish to attend.

The staff who work in the box office have to bear these points in mind when dealing with the thousands of customers. For the Playhouse pantomime two charts are therefore essential. One is the seat-cost chart (see Figure 1) and the other is the seating plan of the theatre.

Production preparation (1)
The preparation for a pantomime obviously has a large part to play in determining its success. Much of the early planning is done by the production committee, who first of all work out the general aims. When they have done this the various experts involved have a better idea of what is required of them.

The general aims for the Harlow Playhouse production of 'Dick Whittington' were:
1 To produce a 'traditional' pantomime without ever losing sight of the fact that the main aim is to entertain.

DECEMBER	DATE	TIME	FULL PRICE			REDUCTIONS		
Tuesday	18	7.30	2.45	2.15	1.65	2.20	1.95	1.40
Wednesday	19	7.30	2.45	2.15	1.65	2.20	1.95	1.40
Thursday	20	7.30	2.45	2.15	1.65	2.20	1.95	1.40
Friday	21	7.30	2.45	2.15	1.65	2.20	1.95	1.40
Saturday	22	3.00	2.45	2.15	1.65	NO REDUCTIONS		
Saturday	22	7.30	2.45	2.15	1.65	NO REDUCTIONS		
Sunday	23		NO PERFORMANCE					
Monday	24		NO PERFORMANCE					
Tuesday	25		NO PERFORMANCE					
Wednesday	26	3.00	2.45	2.15	1.65	NO REDUCTIONS		
Wednesday	26	7.30	2.45	2.15	1.65	NO REDUCTIONS		
Thursday	27	7.30	2.45	2.15	1.65	2.20	1.95	1.40
Friday	28	7.30	2.45	2.15	1.65	2.20	1.95	1.40
Saturday	29	3.00	2.45	2.15	1.65	NO REDUCTIONS		
Saturday	29	7.30	2.45	2.15	1.65	NO REDUCTIONS		
Sunday	30		NO PERFORMANCE					
Monday	31	7.30	2.45	2.15	1.65	2.20	1.95	1.40
JANUARY								
Tuesday	1	3.00	2.45	2.15	1.65	NO REDUCTIONS		
Tuesday	1	7.30	2.45	2.15	1.65	NO REDUCTIONS		
Wednesday	2	7.30	2.45	2.15	1.65	2.20	1.95	1.40
Thursday	3	7.30	2.45	2.15	1.65	2.20	1.95	1.40
Friday	4	7.30	2.45	2.15	1.65	2.20	1.95	1.40
Saturday	5	3.00	2.45	2.15	1.65	NO REDUCTIONS		
Saturday	5	7.30	2.45	2.15	1.65	NO REDUCTIONS		
Sunday	6		NO PERFORMANCE					
Monday	7	7.30	2.45	2.15	1.65	2.20	1.95	1.40
Tuesday	8	7.30	2.45	2.15	1.65	2.20	1.95	1.40
Wednesday	9	7.30	2.45	2.15	1.65	2.20	1.95	1.40
Thursday	10	7.30	2.45	2.15	1.65	2.20	1.95	1.40
Friday	11	7.30	2.45	2.15	1.65	2.20	1.95	1.40
Saturday	12	3.00	2.45	2.15	1.65	NO REDUCTIONS		
Saturday	12	7.30	2.45	2.15	1.65	NO REDUCTIONS		

Figure 1

2 To maintain the traditional approach by means of:

   i)   Clear characters – hero, heroine, villain, Dame, audience's friend, etc.
   ii)   Clear story – not to be lost amidst action, effects, music and comedy.
   iii) Visual appeal – slapstick comedy, magical effects, transformations.
   iv) Perennial, easy-to-understand jokes.
   v)   Music, with the accent on sing-along melody and rhythm.

It is the director of the pantomime who decides what he wants in the first instance and expresses the broad aims. His concern with the overall production led him to include the following note too:

'Technically the show needs to impress, with its shipwreck and "turn again" Whittington scenes. In the outline I've aimed for "high-value" sets, ie, some pieces of carpentry and cloth being lit differently to create an apparent set change. "Magical" effects are part of the villain's act.'

Once the director had expressed his general aims to the production committee they decided on a schedule of meetings and the people who need to be involved. For 'Dick Whittington' the latter included:

production manager – for the team (lighting/sound/design/operation of props)
musical director
artistic director
set designer
costume designer
choreography adviser.

Production preparation (2)

The director of 'Dick Whittington', Barry Bowen, also wrote the script so the first thing to establish in his own mind, and in the minds of the actors and actresses who were to play the parts, was what characters were to be involved and what they should be like. Barry Bowen decided on the following characters, and then made notes of the main characteristics of each.

Cast
Sarah the Cook; King Rat; Dick Whittington; Cat; Alice Fitzwarren; Fitzwarren; Comedians; Fairy Liquid; Captain; Idle Jack; Sultana; Princess, the sultana's daughter; She cat.

Characteristics

SARAH THE COOK	traditional Dame, right down to the plimsolls and football socks. Employed by Fitzwarren, as is Idle Jack who is the butt of her wrath. Involved in all comedy routines.
KING RAT	really bad character with magic powers. His integrity is maintained throughout and although he doesn't succeed in his plans, his bungling is committed by his assistants, rather than himself. *Hiss-boo!*
DICK	the hero, but less of a Prince Charming (immaculate) and more of an Aladdin (slightly impish). He is involved in some comedy as well as love scenes. He is not fully aware of his cat's potential and is slightly put upon by others. In love with Alice. Saves the day after the shipwreck (or rather the cat does!).
TOM, THE CAT	much maligned by all, except Dick and the audience. Is involved in a big production number – the dance routine to rid the Sultan of rats. Tom is comic, loveable and agile.
ALICE FITZWARREN	Fitzwarren's daughter and the heroine. Whilst never losing her audience appeal as the heroine, she is capable of joining in comedy and is more of the 'girl next door' than 'goody two shoes.'
FAIRY LIQUID	a rather outrageous, scatty and absent-minded lady who flits about performing miracles. She is however warm and lovable and eventually 'gets it right.'
COMEDIANS	the two assistants of King Rat, charged to do his dirty work but completely incompetent. At the losing end of the gags and slapstick routines. They turn over a new leaf for the finale but are generally funny, busy, wicked losers.
IDLE JACK	although 'idle' has physically the hardest job in the whole cast, being involved in all the comedy and action scenes and also very active in the dancing numbers. He is the audience's friend, victim of King Rat's plot, and in love with Alice – although he never gets round to doing anything about it.
FITZWARREN	basically a nice old man but 'frugal' with money and easily led by others. His fortune is lost in the shipwreck but regained by Dick.

CAPTAIN   a comedian who makes every entrance with the intention of singing a song, but is always too late or is sent away scornfully. Finally sings his song and impresses the Dame.

SULTANA   small part, supposedly 'all powerful' but actually a 'physical wreck'. Very rich.

PRINCESS   beautiful. Idle Jack's final partner.

SHE CAT   walk-on part only.

Once the characters have been alloted to actors the next important step is to supply them with scripts so that they can learn their lines. At the same time the players need to know what 'action' they are involved in. The director therefore produces a detailed scenario so that all actors and actresses know what is happening, and when. For 'Dick Whittington' the scenario describing the happenings in *Scene 2* looked as follows:

SCENE 2   STREET/SHOP SET – London Town/Fitzwarren's shop
a) Chorus
– Big, opening 'production number' (London Town)
– Song and dance. As each character is introduced, he/she sings a verse, everyone joins in the chorus
– Idle Jack
– Sarah
– Fitzwarren
– Alice
b) Idle Jack establishes report with audience ('wake-up Jack' routine – love for Alice)
c) Recurrent comedy item (Captain's song) (fails)
d) Comedians attempt kidnap of Alice – Whittington rescues her.
   Love scene Whittington and Alice (two-part song). 'Find you a job in our shop' plot
e) Sarah's scene, with Whittington, Cat, Idle Jack – includes shopping routine
f) Fitzwarren and Whittington scene – Whittington gets job
g) Fairy – all appears to be going well

STREET/SHOP SET – At night
a) King Rat's entrance
– plot to plant money on Whittington
b) Comedy scene in shop
– stealing the money; the attempted corruption of Jack

Production preparation (3)

Every bit as important as the preparation of the cast, is the technical preparation for the production. For the Playhouse's production of 'Dick Whittington' the number of people involved in the technical team far outnumbered the members of the cast who actually appeared on stage.

Work on the sets, for instance, involved approximately six weeks of workshop time. The sets required very skilful carpentry and detailed painting. Costumes required the attention of the wardrobe mistress, cutter and fitter, and when they were ready, 'photo calls' had to be arranged so that publicity photographs could be taken.

Whilst all this was going on Cliff Dix, Technical and Stage Manager, had to work out all the special effects and lighting. To do this he had to take into account the backstage facilities – the grid, the fly tower and (in the Playhouse's case) the 33 flying bars which carry the lights (see Figure 2).

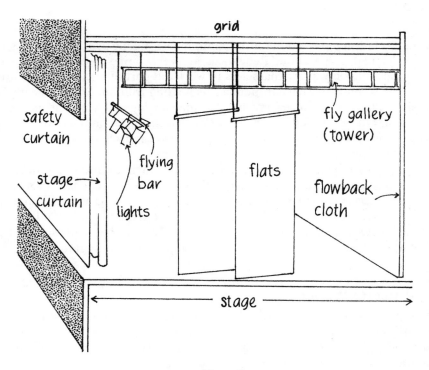

Figure 2

The fly tower is much higher than the stage which is seen by the audience. The grid is the area from which 'flats' for scene changes, backcloths, flying bars, and ropes for manipulation hang. Backstage crews operate all these things.

Once the various effects have been worked out the stage manager controls operations at the performances. He wears a set of headphones to keep him in contact with backstage crew all over the theatre. Set at various parts of the stage and theatre are lighting boxes which have a red and green light on them. These positions are manned by crew members. When the stage manager wants the crew to act in some pre-arranged way the red light on their box goes on, this means 'get ready'; when it is replaced by the green light it means *Action!* At the back of the auditorium is another control room with a large console in it. Some of the pre-arranged lighting is computerised and the details are fed into this console which then controls the lighting automatically.

Cliff Dix's job therefore requires very skilful technical preparation and the utmost attention to detail.

Rehearsals

As the technical preparation for the pantomime is taking place the cast begin more detailed preparation. Rehearsals are very varied indeed. Some are small, needing only a few characters to work out part of a scene; others are extensive when a spectacular 'number' is nearing fruition. Some rehearsals involve talking only; others involve dancing, singing and action sequences. A time has to be decided on when *No Books* is the order on the information sheet. This means that the actors and actresses are expected to know all their words by this time without relying on their scripts.

As well as rehearsal activities being varied, their location also differs. Sometimes, because the action is small the cast do not need to use the stage; on other occasions the stage might be in use by one group and so not available for another one. All of these things are summed up in a rehearsal schedule which is distributed to everyone involved in the pantomime. The rehearsal schedule for 'Dick Whittington' appeared as in Figure 3.

The performance

December 18 and the months of hard work and preparation were about to be put to the test. Both the beautifully-decorated foyer and bar areas were crowded with customers when I arrived at the theatre at 7 pm, half an hour before the curtain was due to go up for the first performance of 'Dick Whittington.' The audience was obviously going to be made up of a mixture of adults and children of all ages and there was a definite feeling of excitement in the air.

PANTO REHEARSAL SCHEDULE

More detailed timings will be given in advance where possible. Please wear clothes suitable for dance at ALL rehearsals, even if not specific 'Dance' rehearsal.
NO BOOKS from 14 November.
Weekdays 7.30 – 10, Sundays 10 – 1, 3 – 6

DATE	CAST	REHEARSAL	VENUE
11 OCTOBER	All	Reading and discussion	Committee room
28 a.m.	All	Songs	School
p.m.		Plot – Act 1	
30	All	Plot – Act 2	Laundry
31	Comics and chorus	Routins	Restaurant
2 NOVEMBER	Principals	Work – Act 1	Restaurant
4 a.m.	All	Songs	School
p.m.	Principals	Work – Act 2	
7	Comics and chorus	Routines	Restaurant
9	All	Dance	Restaurant
11 a.m. ⎱	All	Dance	School
p.m. ⎰		Songs	
14	Principals	Work – Act 1	Restaurant
16	Principals	Work – Act 2	Restaurant
18 a.m.	All	Song and dance	School
p.m.			
21	All	Run Act 1	Restaurant
23	All	Run Act 2	Restaurant
25 a.m. ⎱	All	Run show	School
p.m. ⎰			
28	Principals	Work bits	Restaurant
30	Principals	Work bits	Restaurant
2 DECEMBER			
a.m. ⎱	All	Run Show	Restaurant
p.m. ⎰			
3	All	Run show	Restaurant
5	T.B.A.	T.B.A.	Restaurant
7	T.B.A.	T.B.A.	Restaurant
9 a.m. ⎱	All	Run show	Stage
p.m. ⎰			
10	All	Run show	Stage
11	All	Run show	Stage
12	All	Run show	Stage
14	All	Tech.	Stage
16 a.m.	All	Tech. dress rehearsal	Stage
p.m.	All	Dress rehearsal	Stage
17	All	Public dress rehearsal	Stage
18	All	1st performance	Stage

Figure 3

The 'air' surrounding those who were involved in the show was very different. There was a pre-occupation about their comments and tension was most apparent. Anne Mottershead was feverishly busy with the many last-minute organisational details and Cliff Dix, despite a superficially relaxed demeanour was obviously thinking about how the many extremely complicated lighting and scenic effects would work out.

I took my seat in the auditorium with another person who had been involved with the production since its earliest days. This was Brian Miller, designer of the sets. We made only desultory conversation until the pit orchestra struck up an opening medley of toe-tapping tunes, and then the curtain rose.

The next three hours were interesting in a number of ways. First of all there was the enjoyment engendered by any live, colourful and well-produced show; secondly, there was the additional bonus of being able to view the performance knowing what had gone on in preparation and what was currently going on behind the scenes; thirdly, there was the great advantage of having an expert with me who could give me extra pointers to consider. All these three areas provided much food for thought.

To begin with, seen purely as a member of the audience, the show was a great success. The aims described in *Production preparation (1)* were met absolutely in full. The characters were very clearly delineated and the story

Dick Whittington

CAST IN ORDER OF APPEARANCE

King Rat	*A wicked villain*	**BARRY WALSH**
Fairy Liquid	*A good fairy*	**DORIS PALMER**
Tom, the Cat	*He's nice*	**NICOLE WALTON**
Dick Whittington	*Our hero*	**JANE MILES**
Idle Jack	*A sleepy boy*	**ANDY HAMILTON**
Sarah	*Fitzwarren's Cook*	**KEITH ROWLEY**
Fitzwarren	*An Alderman*	**GORDON HEWLETT**
Alice Fitzwarren	*Our heroine*	**CHRIS MOSLEY**
Itch	*Nearly wicked*	**RON COZZI**
Scratch	*Just as wicked*	**GARY SPICER**
Captain Wormseye	*A sea captain*	**TONY WILSON**
Princess Leila	*Sultana's daughter*	**WENDY HESLOP**
Guard	*He's powerful*	**PATRICK ROBERTS**
Sultana	*Ruler of Morocco*	**KATE HARRIS**
She Cat	*She's nice, too!*	**JOCELYN HEWLETT**

CHORUS
Dancers Extraordinaire
**AMANDA DAVIDGE, JENNY GODWARD,
WENDY HESLOP, JEANNE KELLY,
EMMA TAVERNER, CHLOE TREEND,
TOBY GUNN, STUART MILLER,
SEAN O'SULLIVAN**

'rolled' crisply. The visual effects were outstanding with the London Town scene, the shipwreck and the setting for the finale being superb. The costumes throughout were apt, colourful and spectacular. The jokes were naive (Where's the front of the ship? – At the sharp end; Where's the back? – At the blunt end; Where's the cargo? – In the garage.) by deliberate policy and were appreciated by parents keen to avoid 'smut.' The music was of 'standard-type' pop with a nice touch of jazz to it, and it owed much to an extremely-accomplished organist and pianist.

For me, one of the most interesting things was to see how the 'paper' characters (see *Production preparation (2)*) had developed into real-life creatures. There were some surprises here with some having a more powerful effect than I had envisaged in the overall end product. Idle Jack for instance, by means of looks, demeanour, acrobatic skills and natural charm, established a tremendous rapport with all age groups in the audience. The two bungling evil characters had many first-class scenes but King Rat, a superbly-costumed, agile and threatening villain made only a fraction of the impact I had expected – an indication that the modern child is much more blasé about horror and sinister figures perhaps? Sarah the Cook held the whole show together with boisterous good humour, allowing Dick and Alice to share the 'chocolate box' scenes as a tranquil contrast.

MUSICAL NUMBERS

Act I
Overture

ondon Town	DICK
ne Smile At A Time	PRINCIPALS & CHORUS
tzwarrens	SARAH
ing Bad	ITCH & SCRATCH
on't Stop Me I'm In Love	DICK & ALICE
hittington Out	PRINCIPALS & CHORUS
ew Tomorrow	DICK, ALICE & CHORUS

Act II
Entr'acte

ne To Wave Goodbye	PRINCIPALS & CHORUS
st One Thing Nice	IDLE JACK
eaming	ALICE
on't Stop Me (Reprise)	DICK & ALICE
kin' Over	KING RAT & FAIRY LIQUID
ø Cat Tom	IDLE JACK
nale	THE COMPANY

MUSICIANS
DOUGLAS ADDEY *(Organ)*
JOY ALCOCK *or* **DUNCAN LANE** *(Piano)*
DARREN SALISBURY *(Drums)*

Brian Miller focussed my attention on various other aspects of the production. Having attended many rehearsals it was immediately obvious to him how the cast had to adjust their timing to cater for applause, audience participation and sometimes unexpected responses from the audience. There was also the promise of the 'unexpected' when Idle Jack had six child members of the audience up on the stage with him and was asking them questions.

From a set designer's point of view Brian was most concerned about why one backcloth did not fully reach the stage at one part of the show – a factor which ordinary audience members would not have noticed. He also drew my attention to a magnificent car which he and his team had created and which had taken a great deal of time and work to perfect. Unfortunately, it appeared at a very low key part of the show and certainly did not get the attention it warranted.

At the end of the performance it was revealing to listen to the comments of the audience as they left the theatre. I asked one or two for their opinions about the show and got some very perceptive answers. Children were unanimous in their enthusiasm, with Idle Jack topping the popularity list of almost all age groups. The adults I spoke to were, in the main, very pleased that it was an 'ideal sort of show' for the children they had brought with them. They all thought that the spectacle of the show had been first class, and most were agreed that the cast did a good job in offering something for adults as well as children. With regard to the former, the Sultana, a brilliantly-portrayed Mrs Thatcher lookalike and talkalike, had been particularly appreciated. Several people felt that whilst the visual spectacle had been beyond criticism, the cast would improve on their first performance. Everyone I spoke to felt that they had had excellent value for money and a thoroughly enjoyable night's entertainment.

Conclusion

From a teacher's point of view I felt the whole experience of 'getting behind the scenes' at a pantomime was a very rewarding one. It emphasised how important it is to draw up clear and careful aims when planning a school production; the need to put down on paper the expected characteristics of the parts in the production; the importance of producing a proper scenario into which all components can be fitted.

As a final point, I think schools which are situated near to theatres would find a visit backstage extremely interesting. Based on my experience at Harlow, and what the professionals there told me, theatres often respond most favourably when approached in this context.

Chapter 8

It happened in December

This chapter looks at some of the events and anniversaries connected with the month of December. The aim has been to select things of interest to children which could be developed by teachers.

December and its anniversaries

December takes its name from the Latin term *decem*, meaning ten. This is because it was originally the tenth month of the Roman calendar. During this month the great Roman festival of Saturnalia took place. Saturnus was an ancient god, father of Jupiter, Pluto, Neptune and Nero – and also the god of seed. During December the winter solstice takes place, and the Romans prayed to Saturn to protect the winter-sown crops, and ultimately bring forth a fruitful yield. Thus a most important festival came into being. It was a time of much celebration. Work was abandoned for a week, slaves freed, punishments suspended, presents exchanged, food and drink enjoyed. When Christianity began to spread and a fixed time to celebrate Christ's birth was sought, the winter solstice was chosen. Thus the celebratory traditions of Saturnalia/December/Christ's birth were maintained from the fourth century onwards.

The Anglo-Saxon traditions of December were that it was the last month of the Anglo-Saxon year and went under the descriptive title of Wintermonath, whilst often being linked with the first month of the New Year – Giuli (Yule). Following the spread of Christianity, Wintermonath was sometimes replaced with the word Halighmonath (Holy Month).

As the dreariest month of the year from a Northern European climatic point of view, December has not wanted for poets to describe this aspect of it:

'The melancholy days are come,
The saddest of the year.'

At the same time its great traditions of shared warmth and companionship at home are reflected with equal fervour:

'Whilst I have a home and can do as I will,
December may rage over ocean and hill.'

Multi-cultural anniversaries

Whilst Christmas dominates December in this country to a large extent, there are also many other interesting anniversaries which take place during the month. Some of these can be linked directly to the festival, others offer possibly fruitful diversions which teachers might pursue when considering the month as a whole.

Some of the anniversaries here have been considered in greater depth in Chapter 6. They are included now simply as reminders.

Advent Sunday — the nearest Sunday to 30 November.

Chanukkah   — the eight-day Jewish Festival of Light which begins in the Jewish month of Kislev (overlapping November/December).

Whilst Sikh anniversaries vary because of the use of the Indian Bikrani calendar, two important ones which often fall in December are the martyrdom of Guru Tegh Bahadur, and the birthday of Guru Gobind Singh.

Bodhi Day   — this important Buddhist celebration coincides with the 8 December.

Both Hindu and Shinto celebrations are observed in Japan where homes are cleaned in preparation for New Year (this activity starts on 13 December), and bells are rung at the *Joya No Kane* festivities on 31 December.

Regular, and more familiar festive anniversaries during the month are 6 December – St Nicholas; 13 December St Lucia; 31 December Hogmanay.

Perhaps less well-known is the belief that the last Monday in December was supposedly the birthday of Judas Iscariot.

Anniversaries – political/historical/people

It should be noted in this section that the 'Ref:' comments are simply suggestions which might be helpful to teachers in forming links with Christmas.

December
1   1942   First publication of the Beveridge Report, the foundation stone of Britain's welfare state
(Ref: better Christmases for the majority)
     1919   Nancy Astor became the first woman MP

689 Death of St Eligius – patron saint of miners, taxi-drivers, farmers and jockeys

2 1804 Napoleon Bonaparte crowned Emperor of First French Empire by Pope Pius VII

1963 A telephone cable 9 000 miles long was laid from Australia to Canada – the world's longest submarine telephone cable.
(Ref: communications with distant relatives and friends)

1859 John Brown (commemorated in the song 'John Brown's body lies a moulderin' in the grave') was hanged in Charleston, Virginia, USA. His great dream to obtain freedom for slaves had failed.
(Ref: Christmas as a time of compassion)

3 1894 Death of Robert Louis Stevenson:
'The world is so full of a number of things
I'm sure we should all be as happy as kings.'
(Ref: use of words, songs, poems at Christmas time)

1795 Birth date of Rowland Hill, he introduced the postage stamp in 1840.
(Ref: cards, parcels, letters at Christmas)

4 1865 Birth date of Edith Cavell – the nurse who was shot by the Germans during the First World War for helping British soldiers to escape.
(Ref: 'sacrifice' at Christmas)

5 1791 Death of Mozart
(Ref: music at Christmas)

6 342 Death of St Nicholas, Bishop of Myra, the original 'Santa Claus.' Not many facts are known about St Nicholas and even the year of his death is uncertain. His standing as the parton saint of the young has been well-established for hundreds of years – perhaps particularly because of one legend which tells how he pulled three small children from a tub in which they were being pickled to death. His feast day is strongly kept in continental Europe. He also has associations with the sea and sailors.

Seventeenth-century Dutch immigrants took 'Sinter Klaus' with them to America, where he eventually became 'Santa Claus.'
(For further reference to St Nicholas, see Chapter 2, page 20.)

7 1941 Japanese attacked Pearl Harbour, thus bringing the United States of America into the Second World War.
(Ref: Christmas as a time to think of, and pray for, peace)

8 1660 First actress appeared on British stage. Before this all female parts had been played by boys.
(Ref: Christmas pantomimes – principal 'boys', 'dames', etc.)
65 Birth date of Roman poet Horace who often wrote about love, care, thought for others and friendship.

9 1921 Death of Arthur Pearson, founder of St Dunstan's Home for the Blind, and a man who realised the value of taking poor city children out to enjoy the country.
(Ref: Christmas as a time for thinking of, and doing something about, those less fortunate than ourselves)

10 1896 Death of Alfred Nobel – founder of the five annual prizes presented for great work in the sciences, literature and the service of peace. The prizes were first presented in 1901.
(Ref: Christmas – a wider look at 'gifts')

11 1688 James II left the throne

12 1889 Death of Robert Browning ('The Pied Piper of Hamelin')
(Ref: Christmas – a time of promises, how they should be kept)
1901 Marconi's great achievement – the transmission of the first morse signal across the Atlantic. The signal was the letter 'S'.
(Ref: Christmas – how we have benefited from inventions)

13 304 St Lucia martyred in 304, in Sicily. She was executed for helping Christians. She is remembered particularly in Sweden, where girls wearing wreaths of candles on their heads distribute ginger biscuits. The original St Lucia lit her way with candles round her head, leaving her hands free to take food to refugee Christians.

14 1503 Nostradamus was born. One of the most famous of astrologers, Nostradamus predicted what would happen to, and in, the world in future centuries.
(Ref: Christmas horoscopes — particularly for those children whose birth signs are Sagittarius, the Centaur (23 November

to 22 December), and Capricorn, the Goat (23 December to
21 January)

15 1832 Birth date of Alexandre Eiffel, designer of the 300-metre high
tower in Paris.

1860 Birth date of James Murrell. A magician who claimed he
could see into the future, he also specialised in finding lost
property by looking for its whereabouts in his 'magic mirror.'
(Ref: Christmas links with magic, jokes and tricks)

16 1770 Birth date of Beethoven

1775 Birth date of Jane Austen

1859 Death of Wilhelm Grimm (of the brothers' Grimm)

1882 Birth date of Jack Hobbs, England cricketer
(Ref: Useful pointers for discussing the talents which give
pleasure at Christmas)

1911 Amundsen reached the South Pole

17 1903 First aeroplane flight by Orville Wright in Kittyhawk, North
Carolina, USA. The flight lasted for 12 seconds.
(Ref: communications at Christmas)

18 1865 Slavery was abolished in USA
(Ref: links with John Brown and Christmas compassion)

19 1981 This was the date of the Penlee Lifeboat disaster. A ship
called the *Union Star* got into difficulties off Land's End. The
Penlee Lifeboat, crewed by men from the Cornish village of
Mousehole, set off to help. In winds of 80 knots the lifeboat
capsized and eight lifeboatmen were lost.
(Ref: Christmas – life, and danger, in the service of others
goes on at all times)

20 On this date in 1879, Thomas Edison gave the first demonstra-
tion of an electric lamp.
(Ref: light at Christmas)

21 St Thomas's Day. A first-century apostle who spread the
gospel in the Middle and Far East and who was killed in India,
he is sometimes remembered by the ringing of bells on this
day. Bell ringing is also associated with the beginning of the
Christmas festival and the 'ringing-in of Christmas.'

22

In some countries Christmas has stayed a legal as well as a traditional holiday and anniversary, in spite of changes of government to those who officially despise all religious activities. This occasionally leads to strange pronouncements, such as the following which was issued in Czechoslovakia on this date:

> 'Because Christmas Eve will fall on a Thursday, that day will be considered a Saturday for work purposes. Factories will be closed all day, although stores will remain closed a half-day only. Friday, December 25, will be considered a Sunday. Monday, December 28, will be a Wednesday for work purposes. Wednesday will be a business Friday, Saturday will be a Sunday, and Sunday will be a Monday.'

(Ref: How Christmas has for so long and so often surmounted the changes and affairs of man. Link also with the Puritans banning of Christmas in England between 1642 and 1660)

23 1952

Frenchman Alain Bombard landed in the West Indies after choosing to spend 65 days on an inflatable life raft in the Atlantic. His courage and endurance have since saved many lives because his ideas on survival have been taught to many sailors.

(Ref: Christmas – the gift of life and the need to work at sustaining it)

24

Christmas Eve and . . . the first Festival of Nine Lessons and Carols at King's College, Cambridge, was held in 1918. At the parish church of Dewsbury, Yorkshire, bells are tolled for every year that has passed since the birth of Christ – this practice has been taking place for over seven hundred years.

25

Midnight mass heralds Christmas day in most Christian countries. The tradition of present giving precedes the Christian era as the Romans exchanged gifts during the festival of Saturnalia: honey symbolised a peaceful year; candles a year full of happiness and light; money a year of prosperity.

26

Boxing day owes its name to the fact that the contents of the church poor boxes used to be opened and distributed on 26 December. This is also St Stephen's Day. Stephen was an early Christian, a forceful speaker, and a man always concerned for those in need. Arrested and brought before the

Sanhedrin he was ordered to denounce Christianity or be sentenced to death. He refused to give up his religion and was stoned to death, thus becoming the first Christian martyr in AD 33.
(Ref: the true significance of Chrsitmas and what Christianity has meant to some people)

27 100 St John died, and this is the day on which he is remembered. Most of his life was spent preaching and writing.

28 The feast day of St Wenceslas – patron saint of Bohemia, 'Good King Wenceslas,' (For further reference see Chapter 2 p. 27)

This date also commemorates Holy Innocents' Day. When King Herod heard of the birth of a new king in Bethlehem he determined to protect his position by having all boys of two years and under killed. In this way he was sure the 'new king' would be caught up in the slaughter. Jesus, along with Mary and Joseph, had already escaped to Egypt but this day is in memory of those children who were killed.

December 28 has also long held a reputation of being an 'unlucky' day and any new venture or speculation should be delayed until it has passed.

29 St Thomas Becket's day. After the misunderstanding which led to his death, Thomas Becket was declared a saint and martyr.

30 1865 Birth of Rudyard Kipling in Bombay
(Ref: pleasure of words at Christmas)

31 New Year's Eve and of little significance in church traditions. The idea of New Year resolutions is well summed up by Charles Lamb:

'Every first of January that we arrive at, is an imaginary milestone on the turnpike track of human life; at once a resting place for thought and meditation and a starting point for fresh exertion in the performance of our journey. The man who does not at least propose to himself to be better this year than he was last, must be either very good or very bad indeed.'

(Ref: Christmas – a time when we try to see the 'best' in everybody)

Chapter 9

Christmas craft

As all teachers know the demand for craft ideas at Christmas is never ending. The aim in this chapter is to provide some easy to do, inexpensive suggestions. They are basic but could be increased in complexity if dealing with older, more able children.

Make your own real Christmas tree

Many schools display a real, or artificial, Christmas tree in the foyer or hall during the build-up to the festival. Whilst this provides a dramatic focal point, few children feel that it is 'their' tree. The latter feeling can only really be achieved by having a tree in the classroom. This is not such a difficult task if a little careful forethought is used. Many trees, relics of Christmases past, have been planted in gardens and reach enormous heights. One in the school where I work dominates an open quadrangle from a height of about eighteen feet.

It is these trees from which materials for other 'real' Christmas trees can be taken. Following the directions set out below should help.

1　Select a base to contain the tree. This should be a heavy container and could be filled with either soil, or a block of foam plastic, or water covered with a fairly large mesh wire netting.

2　Select some branches from a garden-growing tree. The best and most obvious to take are those near the bottom, and one of the branches should be bigger than the other two or three. Once the branches have been chosen they should be arranged in a tree shape and tied together with florists' wire.

This should be done as carefully as possible to give a good shape, and the tree should then be put in the container.

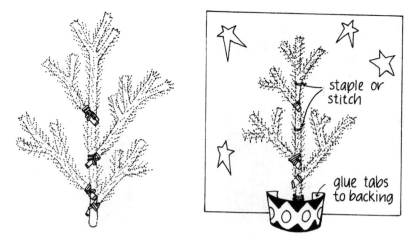

Figure 1

3   The next step is to prevent the needles dropping from the branches and this can be achieved by brushing them with a solution of wallpaper paste.
4   The tree can then be garlanded with whatever is chosen. A further advantage is that branches can be added or taken away as required.

Some classrooms of course are small and overcrowded and difficult places in which to find space to stand a tree. In this case the tree can be wall-mounted. Once again the branches should be selected and treated. An appropriate backing material should then be put on a wall. Next, a painted and decorated 3D – base should be put in place, and then the tree stitched or stapled into place. Decorations should then be painted on the backcloth, or created in 3D form.

One further possibility for a crowded room where it is advantageous to 'elevate' the tree is to simply use branches in a wall-mounted arrangement. Each branch can then be decorated individually to give an attractive freize-like appearance.

Hang this

Hanging Christmas decorations look equally attractive in school or home. The following are easy to make.

Baubles

Materials required; pipe cleaners, gold or silver spray, tinsel, card, scissors, pencil

Technique
1 Take two pipe cleaners and join them together in the shape of a circle. Using a gold or silver spray, spray the circle.
2 Take a piece of black card, measure and cut it so that it 'fills' the circle quite substantially (Figure 2).

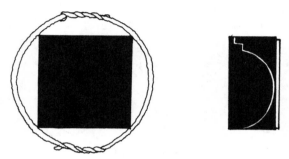

Figure 2

3 Remove the card and fold it in half. Then using a pencil (preferably yellow or white) which shows up on the black colour, draw a half-bauble shape on the card (Figure 3).
4 Keeping the two thicknesses of card together, cut round this shape. When complete, open it out.
5 Next, cut various small shapes from the residue of the card and lay them on one side of the shape. Using the same coloured spray as has been used on the pipe cleaners, spray over the shapes. When dry, take the cut-out shapes off and repeat the process on the other side.
6 Make a small hole in the top of the bauble shape and fasten it with tinsel to the pipe cleaner. Then, with another piece of tinsel hang the shape where required.

Figure 3

Glittering baubles

Materials required: some old table tennis balls, a spray of gold paint, glue, brown sugar, tinsel

Technique
1 Spray the table tennis balls with gold paint.
2 When the paint is dry smear them with glue.
3 Roll them in brown sugar.
4 Stick a piece of tinsel on each one and hang them up.

Dangling Pasta

Materials required: collection of various shapes of pasta, brightly-coloured paint or spray, tinsel string

Technique
1 Thread the pieces of pasta on pieces of tinsel.
2 Spray or paint with bright colours.
3 Display on the tree or around the room.

Pleasing parcels

Materials required: collection of small to 'smallish' boxes, eg, matchboxes, empty containers of various household items, glue, collection of brightly-coloured wrappers (eg, from biscuits and sweets)

Technique
1 Flatten and press all the colourful wrappers.
2 Smear the boxes with glue.
3 Cover the boxes in bright wrappers.
4 Display at the foot of the Christmas tree.

Nutty clumps

Materials required: collection of various shapes of pasta, brightly-coloured paint or spray, tinsel string

Technique
1 Spray the nuts and cones with silver/gold paint.
2 Mix plaster of paris with water and pour the mixture into the lid containers.
3 Set nuts and cones, along with a few sprigs of holly into plaster of paris to make attractive table decorations.

Bright berries

Materials required: collection of buttons and beads from any sewing box, thread, green or red spray paint

Technique
1 Spray the buttons and beads and allow them to dry.
2 Thread into 'clumps.'
3 Hang from the Christmas tree or around room.

Gift containers

Materials required: collection of bottles, papier mâché, paint, varnish, squeezy washing-up liquid bottle

Technique
1 Make some variously-shaped papier mâché 'heads' and attach them to the bottles.

Figure 4

2 Allow the heads to dry thoroughly and make sure they are adhering firmly. Then put a thin layer of papier mâché over all of the bottle.
3 When dry, paint the bottles. When paint is dry apply a coat of varnish.
4 Make a mixture of three parts interior Polyfilla and two parts water. Make sure all lumps have been eliminated and then put into the squeezy bottle. If required, some powder paint could be added to the mixture.
5 Pipe the mixture from squeezy bottle onto the painted and prepared 'gift' bottles. The piping could be done indiscriminately, or it could be used to form a mesh to make the end products look like 'flagons.' (The better 'flagons' are useful for drama – as in gifts given by the Wise Men.)

Figure 5

Easy mosaics

There are many ways of producing mosaic pictures – using paper cut from glossy magazines, crepe paper, materials, seeds, pasta. However, one of the easiest and most effective for young children is to use eggshells.

Materials required: eggshells, dyes, contrasting coloured cards, paper, pencil, glue

Technique
1 Dye the eggshells and let them dry. When this has been done they should be broken up into small pieces. Different colours could be put into different piles.
2 A piece of card should be selected for the base of the mosaic and a contrasting coloured card superimposed on this. These should then be glued together, and a place for the name of the 'artist' should be provided.

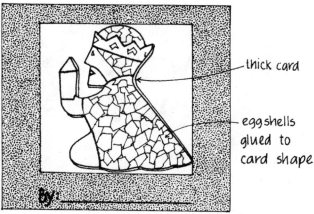

thick card

eggshells glued to card shape

Figure 6

3   A simple picture shape should be decided upon, and drawn on a piece of paper. Next, cut round the outline of the picture and stick it onto the card.

4   There are then two ways of decorating the picture. It might be divided by a series of simple line divisions; different coloured eggshells could then be stuck in each of the sections. Alternatively the eggshells could be stuck on indiscriminately without regard for any arranged pattern. Whichever method is used it should be noted that the easiest way to stick on the eggshells is to 'paint' the figure with glue and then simply stick shell where desired.

Christmas plaques

Christmas plaques, made by older juniors, have various virtues. When done well they look quite sophisticated; they are unusual and attractive items to display; they can be sold for fund-raising purposes.

Materials required: a selection of box lids, polythene, interior Polyfilla, a lino knife or other V-shaped tool, a sealant (for example, emulsion paint), a selection of old wax crayons and the means to melt them

Technique

1   Line a box lid with polythene. Make a smooth mixture of Polyfilla, pour this into the lid and gently shake until the Polyfilla is level. Then it should be left to dry.

2   With the lino tool cut the required engraving into the Polyfilla. A sensible precaution is to pencil in the lines to be cut first.

Figure 7

3 After the surplus material has been brushed away from the grooves a sealing mixture should be applied to them. A small amount of emulsion paint is useful for this.
4 Next, melt the wax crayons and use the molten wax to fill in the grooves which have been cut in the cast.
5 When the wax has hardened the cast could be removed from its box lid and fixed onto a piece of thick card or hardboard to give it a more finished appearance.

Christmas bells

Materials required: yogurt pots, cartons which have held glace cherries etc., ribbons, string, plasticine, powder paint

Technique
1 Paint the pots and let them dry.
2 Put a ribbon through the base of each pot. On the inside attach a piece of plasticine which looks like the clanger of a bell.
3 Hang pots as 'bells'.

Life-size 'models'

Materials required: card, scissors, sellotape, paint, balaclava or stocking top

Technique
1 Place a large piece of card on the floor and ask one child to lie on it. The card must stretch from shoulders to ankles.
2 Paint the card. When the paint is dry, bend the card into a cylindrical shape and tape the sides together. Stick top on cylinder and cut out a hole for the wearer's head.
3 If the model is to be, say, a 'life-sized candle', the next thing is to prepare its 'flame' by taking another piece of card and painting it a mixture of red/yellow/orange. This should have eye holes for the wearer to see through and an elastic band inserted so that it can be held round the head.
4 Before the 'flame' is put on, the subject should put on a dark balaclava or stocking top to represent the wick. The end product of all this would then appear as shown overleaf.
5 This costume can of course be adapted for many other life-sized shapes which might be required, particularly for dramatic presentations at this time of the year.

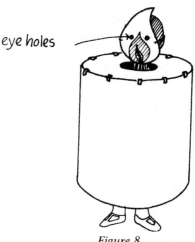

eye holes

Figure 8

'What lovely paper!'

The presentation of presents in attractive wrapping paper is pleasing to the receiver and giver, and the making of such paper is both an enjoyable and rewarding experience for children. It is also a relatively easy and inexpensive exercise as the following examples illustrate.

Marbled paper

Materials required: large tray, a little oil, paint, stick, cold water, paper

Technique
1   Half fill the tray with cold water.
2   Add a very small quantity of oil and some drops of different coloured paints.
3   Stir carefully with a stick to give the colours a 'whorled' effect.
4   Lay pieces of paper, one at a time, on the surface of this oil/paint mix. Give them a few seconds to 'take', then remove and dry.
5   The end product should be attractive, professional looking wrapping paper.

Rubbed paper

Materials required: card, paper, scissors, glue, wax crayons

Technique
1   Decide on a design and draw it on thick card. Cut out the shape and stick it on a larger piece of card to give a slight 3D effect.

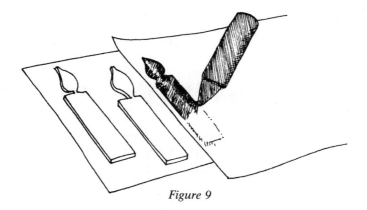

Figure 9

2   Fix the 'wrapping paper' over the card and 'rub it' with a wax crayon. As the wrapping paper will probably be larger than the card the rubbing should either be a section at a time, or at random. It is important to ensure that the overlay is stable when the rubbing is taking place.
3   Different coloured paper could be used and particularly effective crayon colours for this purpose are gold, silver, red and green.

A flock of sheep

Materials required: cotton wool, empty cotton reels, pipe cleaners, black paint, glue

Technique
1   Attach pipe cleaners to the cotton reels to make horns and legs.
2   Stick cotton wool overall to form heads and bodies. Put in eyes and hooves with touches of black paint.

twist horns through legs

twist   twist

cotton wool

black paint

Figure 10

Cork faces

Materials required: corks, toilet roll insides, glue, paint, pieces of fabric, wool, pins, crepe paper

Technique
1   Paint toilet rolls to look like 'bodies' for example, Father Christmas, a soldier, a queen.
2   Stuff the tube with crepe paper.
3   Decorate a cork with materials glued to it to make a 'face.'
4   Insert the cork into the top of the toilet roll so that it rests on crepe paper. Insert a pin from either side to pierce the toilet roll and hold the 'head' in place. eg:

Figure 11

Magic lanterns

Making these involves both fire and nails so they should obviously not be attempted without teacher supervision and presence. The end products however make very attractive lights on gloomy afternoons, and there is the re-assuring safety factor that if they are knocked over they go out immediately.

Materials required: some candle stubs, nails, jam jars, water, matches, paint

Technique
1   Dip a paint brush containing a different colour of paint into several jam jars, three-quarters full of water, to make a blue jar, red jar, green jar, etc.
2   Stick a nail into the base of the candle stubs and the place these in the

water, where they will float. (Some experimentation with nails may be necessary to get the weight right.)
3 Light the candle. As the flame burns the candle down it will rise in the water – thus keeping the flame above the water level.

Half and half

This activity provides an opportunity for children to produce a surprise present to take home.

Materials required: pencils (or charcoal or Indian ink), scissors, some old magazines, a fairly large photograph of a member of the child's family or one of him/herself, sellotape, card

Technique
1 Make a selection of full face photographs from the magazines. Distribute these to the children.
2 Fold each photograph in half lengthways, lay it on a piece of drawing paper and anchor it with small pieces of sellotape. Alternatively, anchor the photograph to a larger piece of paper or card, fold a blank sheet of paper in half lengthways and place it over the photograph so that only half the face shows.

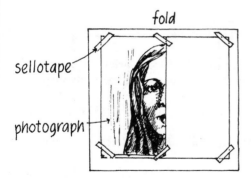

Figure 12

3 Using the features visible as guidelines, draw the missing half of the face. Remove the photograph.
4 Using this 'half' complete the picture so that a full face drawing now appears on the sheet.
5 This exercise so far has been a preliminary to the reproduction of somebody in each child's family. This is done by laying a family photograph on a sheet of paper and 'blanking off' one half of the face without bending or defacing the photograph in any way. Both halves are then finished off as previously described.

6   When the portrait or self portrait has been completed it could be carefully stuck onto a piece of card to give it a framed effect. It is then ready to be given as a surprise Christmas present.

Print a Christmas card

Apart from being fun to do, printing Christmas cards gives them a little touch of the unusual. The idea which follows allows for some very simple work which can be added to by children who are more capable.

Materials required: lino, lino cutting tools – preferably a box of assorted cutting blades with handles, printing ink, paper, glass on which to spread ink, rollers

Technique A
1   Cut a design in the lino block – this can be as simple or as detailed as the capabilities of the children will allow.
2   Spread the ink on the glass and charge the blocks.
3   Print onto the front of prepared folded Christmas cards.

Technique B
This is simply extending the work done in technique A to give a more sophisticated end product.
1   Clean and dry the blocks which have been used in A.
2   Chose three printing ink colours of varying intensity, for example, yellow, green, brown.
3   Spread the glass with yellow, charge the block, print.
4   Clean and dry the block and then cut more out of it to increase the printing pattern.
5   Spread the glass with green, charge the block and print over the first print on the paper.
6   Clean and dry the block, cut out more of it to increase the pattern yet again.
7   Spread the glass with brown, charge the block, print on the paper over the first two prints.

Christmas pictures and posters

Hot and cold

There are few subjects as evocative as Christmas for promoting pictures which are either 'warm' or 'cold.' Indoor Christmas pictures, for instance, almost always reflect a warm, firelit, cosy image; those showing outdoor scenes are often of cold, starry, snowy scenes.

Chalks and pastels are very good tools for providing contrasting pictures of this type.

Materials required: a variety of chalks and/or pastels, a fixative, some different coloured, slightly textured paper

Technique

1   The first thing to consider is the linking of the paper base with the chalks to reflect the 'image' required. For an indoor picture red and orange paper will give the best background; for a cold December outdoor picture then blue is obviously the best coloured paper to use.
2   When applying the chalks/pastels to the paper this should always be done firmly and fine lines are obviously less important than bold masses of colour. One of the advantages here is that lines can be blurred and colours mixed to give quite dramatic effects. This is done by rubbing and mixing the edges of the colours with the fingertips. Sweeps of 'winter skies, snowy landscapes, indoor carpets' can be achieved with this technique.
3   When the pictures are finished they must be 'fixed' to avoid unwanted smudging. Fixatives are most easily sprayed on, and hair spray is useful in this context.

Colour and lights

Colour and lights feature in most people's visual ideas of Christmas. They can be combined in a number of ways – lights on a Christmas tree, in a town display, reflected from a pile of parcels, at a party.

A particularly suitable medium for doing pictures showing these things is described as follows.

Materials required: thick paper, wax crayons, powder paint, washing-up liquid, large nails

Technique

1   Using the wax crayons very heavily make a pattern on the paper. Press hard and make sure that no part of the paper is left uncovered.
2   Make a mixture of the powder colour and washing-up liquid. This must be of a consistency which is very thick – like double cream. For the best results a large spoonful of powder paint should be put in a jar and then the washing liquid added and stirred in a little at a time.
3   Once the paint/washing-up liquid is of the right consistency it should be spread thoroughly over the waxed paper.
4   Allow the mix to stick to the wax and then dry out.
5   Once everything is thoroughly dry take the nail and 'cut' a design in the paint/washing-up liquid mix. As the design is cut the wax colours beneath will show through reflecting lines of changing colours and the 'lights' appear.

Make a menorah

For those who have been linking some multi-cultural work with their Christmas activities a relevant, and easy, craft exercise would be to make a menorah. (NB The menorah is a special Jewish candlestick used for the celebration of *Channukah*, see page 75.)

Material required: two toilet roll insides, paper, card, something with which to punch small holes, candles or straws, yellow and red crepe paper, glue, ruler, pencil, compass

Technique

1   Take one of the toilet roll insides. Cover it with coloured paper, sealing both ends. Next, measure off nine equally-spaced points along the co-vered toilet roll. Then punch out holes at these points.

2   Take the card and using a compass draw a circle on it. This must be large enough to form a base for an upended toilet roll. Draw two or three more circles the same size and stick them all together to form a base. From the rest of the card cut a strip the length of the toilet roll and about three centimetres wide.

Alternatively, a base could be made by filling a tin lid with Polyfilla. If this method is chosen remember to insert the toilet roll before the Polyfilla is set.

3   Take the second toilet roll. Cover it with paper in the same manner as the first and in the same colour. Stick this toilet roll to the base which has been made and then stick the card strip along the top.

4   Next, stick the first toilet roll onto the strip.

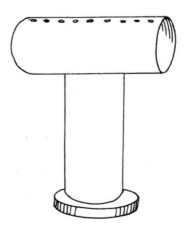

Figure 13

5   If candles are being used then the next step is the insertion of candles of an appropriate size into the holes in the top of the toilet roll. If real candles are not available then models can be made out of covered or painted half straws. Insert small pieces of red and yellow crepe paper into the top of the straws to simulate flames.

IMPORTANT Obviously no attempt should ever be made to light candles in this type of model.

Chapter 10

Christmas incidentals

Perhaps more than any other time of the year the weeks immediately preceding Christmas call for a variety of activities – and create a need for 'incidental' material. The latter can be useful on many occasions – when half the class is at a carol service rehearsal, on the morning before the Christmas party; when bad weather has kept everyone indoors; when staff 'juggling' is necessary for one reason or another.

This chapter therefore offers a pot pourri of ideas, all of which aim to get children involved and interested quickly, and they are all easy to instigate.

It came out of a bottle

Starting with the idea of messages found in bottles some most interesting work in imaginative discussion, writing and drama can ensue. Perhaps the best way to start such a lesson is to ask the children to imagine what sort of situation they might be in to make them send a message in a bottle. Some examples are very useful here and, fortunately, there are plenty of bizarre and interesting ones to choose from.

1   In 1560 Queen Elizabeth I created an official position of 'Uncorker of Bottles!' This was because a fisherman found a bottle on the south coast and, on opening it, discovered a message addressed to the queen from one of her spies. As a result of this all future finds had to be handed over unopened to the 'Uncorker of Bottles.' Anyone opening a bottle on their own accord could be punished by death.

2   The longest recorded journey by a bottle was established in 1929. A scientific expedition put a bottle into the Indian Ocean with a message clearly visible through the glass. This message asked finders to add a note of where and when the bottle was found, and then put it back in the sea. After six years, and reports of finds as far apart as Cape Horn and Western Australia, it had travelled 16 000 miles.

3   The poet Shelley 'bottled' many of his poems in the hope that they would reach a wider audience, and there have been several instances of religious messages and advice being floated off in bottles.
4   One of the most romantic bottle stories concerns a Swedish sailor. In 1956 Ake Viking threw a bottle from his ship. In it was a message asking the finder to give the bottle to a young lady who might write to him. Two years later the bottle was found by a Sicilian fisherman who gave it to his daughter. She wrote to Ake, and eventually married him.

Once this preliminary information has been discussed then it can be given a Christmas link and used to initiate some children's work. The following ideas might be used as starters.

1   'The Unusual Christmas Gift' – a found bottle with a message in it is given as a Christmas gift. Who is it from? What does the message say? What happens?
2   One Christmas an empty bottle has a message of goodwill put in it. It is floated off with an invitation for finders to write to a given address. What happens to the bottle? Describe its adventures and the ultimate consequences.
3   A bottle with a message 'Happy Christmas Dad' is lost one Christmas. How was it lost? What happens to it? Does anybody benefit? Does it get back to the person for whom it is intended?
4   'Father Christmas' decides to float off hundreds of bottles with a message in them. What is the message? Why has he written it? What are the consequences?

With a little imagination the bottle idea could provide plenty of scope for talking and writing and drama. It might also provide some practical adventures!

What happened next?

Starting with the old game of Consequences a structured lesson can be built up which is fun to participate in and which gives considerable practice to imaginative communication skills. All that is needed in the way of equipment is pencils and paper.

1   A pattern of consequences could be worked out. This could be based on the old parlour game – 'He' meets 'She' at X; He said; She said – and the consequences were, etc. It can be pointed out to the children that if we know a little more about 'He' and 'She' this would help to develop the story. This discussion could lead on to the second activity.
2   More details of 'He' might be:

'Oliver Johnson was thirteen years old. For months he had been very miserable at home. Since his father had lost his job there had been endless rows. On Christmas Eve Oliver decided to run away. He went to his bedroom early that night, packed a small case, put all his savings in his wallet and put the light out. When he was sure his parents had gone to bed he crept downstairs and let himself quietly out of the front door. He hurried off to the town station.'

More details of 'She' might be:

'She' is either a young person with whom Oliver has some sort of adventure; an older person who helps Oliver and his parents; an evil person who seeks to trap Oliver; a vulnerable person whom Oliver helps.

When 'He' and 'She' meet, points to consider might be: how does the conversation go and where do they actually meet? Do they already know each other? If not, how do they break the ice as strangers? Do they come to any decisions? What action do they decide to take?

When the 'consequences' are reached do they provide for – a happy ending in which all difficulties are cleared up; an ending in which somebody 'gets their just deserts;' an ending which is really just the beginning of another story; an ending in which 'right' and 'wrong' are clearly seen?

Incidental Christmas mime and drama

Linking Christmas and mime/drama might suggest some interesting subjects for fairly impromptu work.

1   A first consideration might be how you can act wordlessly using only your face, your hands, your body. Portrayals of delight, surprise, sorrow, apprehension, disappointment, excitement, fear, etc., might be attemped.

Next, the activity could be extended so that it relates to people or things even though they may only exist in the imagination. For example:

a) Creeping downstairs on Christmas Eve whilst trying not to wake the rest of the family.

b) Getting a present which is very disappointing – but the recipient does not want to hurt the giver's feelings by showing this.

c) Trying to get a Christmas tree needle out of a cat's foot.

d) Eating a large meal at a party when you have already eaten – but are too embarrassed to tell your host.

e) Trying to control the family dog who goes mad because he sees a toy cat on the Christmas tree.

f) Learning to dance with your new tap shoes (or roller skate, or ride a bicycle, etc.)

g) Mending the window after you kicked the ball you got for Christmas through it.

h) Being a policeman who is investigating crimes whereby a fake Father Christmas is stealing toys.

i) Showing a person who does not speak a work of your language how to use a sledge.

j) Being a car driver who has to get his passengers to the station in time to catch a train – and who is stuck in a traffic jam.

k) Having an expensive ticket to a pantomime, which you cannot find minutes before you are due to leave home.

l) Eating your Christmas dinner when you feel a sudden pain in your mouth and . . . (Use your imagination!)

2 Having participated in a number of mimes like this the next step might be to consider how a group of activities like this might be linked up to form a story. For instance the journey of Mary and Joseph could be a 'starter' here:

a) Receiving the news of the census.
b) Preparing for the journey.
c) What happened on the way.
d) At the outskirts of the city.
e) In the streets of the city.
f) Finding a room.

Features to portray in such a sequence might include: consternation, indignation, resignation, energy, determination, durability, surprise, confusion, anger, concern, irritation, frustration and relief.

Drawings for the non-drawer

The hidden aim of this lesson is to introduce children to a good poem which is well suited to the 'ghostly, dark nights in the house alone' type of atmosphere which December often creates. The obvious aim is to get them to use their imagination in doing 'detective' work to find the places where 'non-drawings' could be used to illustrate the poem.

Obviously the poem used here could be substituted by many others, but it is reproduced here with some examples of the 'non-drawings' which might be used to illustrate it. The children could write out the poem and use their own ideas on illustration as they went along. Comparisons could be interesting.

Coming home

It's not really scary
when you come in the house
and nobody's there

its just
that the chairs seem to
stare
and the room looks so big and
the deep sounds of quiet
make a buzz in your ears

and
Mum'll be back soon
it's really all right
the teapot's all ready

I'm not at all frightened
I'll switch on the TV
but not for a minute

I'll just sit here
I don't want to move from the chair
and it's not really scary
I'm not at all frightened

and only a Baby would start to believe
that something invisible's
sitting behind

I'll look in a minute
Yes, that's what I'll do
in a minute I'll look

I'll just sit here
and soon I'll switch on
the TV

in a minute or two
it's only a box – after all
just a box and I know that

it can't really whisper
those horrible things
when it isn't switched on
      cos
I'm old enough now
Yes, I'm old enough now and
I don't really mind
cos
it's only till six.

Figure 9

Mick Gowar

Palmistry please

All children are interested in themselves and an exercise in reading palms could stimulate much imaginative speculation. At the same time it could enhance vocabulary and discussion – and it is good fun!

1   The first activity is for the children to study their own hands carefully. At the same time some basic information on hands could be put on the blackboard. It could appear as follows:

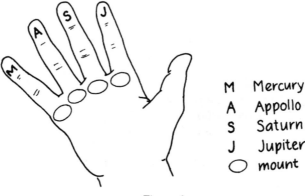

M Mercury
A Appollo
S Saturn
J Jupiter
◯ mount

Figure 1

2   Once hands and the blackboard information have been looked at, the teacher could explain that each finger was named after a Roman god – as shown on the blackboard.

A look at the mounts at the bottom of each finger indicates which of them has the most 'energy' and is therefore the most dominant. Once this has been established reference to the particular characteristics of the god named on each finger reveals the personality of the person owning the hand.

For instance, as it is Christmas, the characteristics of Saturn could be discussed first. A person whose mount shows that the middle finger is the most energetic would be expected to be: a good judge, someone with a strong sense of right and wrong, a person who is always looking for the truth and does a lot of inward thinking.

Main characteristics for the fingers are:

Jupiter   shows the person to be a leader; confident about making decisions; ambitious; possibly a religious person and certainly someone who should make a lot of money.

Apollo   shows the person to be linked to the patron of creative arts; should therefore be artistic, deep thinking and capable of expressing inner feelings to the rest of the world.

Mercury   shows the person to be very good at communicating with others; very good at forming relationships with other people and always diplomatic.

3   Once the preceding information has been absorbed and discussed, a further activity could be for each child to write some comment which supports the characteristics denoted by the dominant finger.

Number fun

Following on the 'subjective' enjoyment of the palmistry activity a useful follow-up is for children to find out even more about themselves by reference to their 'lucky numbers.' There are several ways to find these but the one which could be used here would require the following to be written on the blackboard:

A	B	C	D	E	F	G	H	I	J	K	L	M
1	2	3	4	5	6	7	8	9	1	2	3	4

N	O	P	Q	R	S	T	U	V	W	X	Y	Z
5	6	7	8	9	1	2	3	4	5	6	7	8

It will then be apparent from this that each letter has a number value. A name could then be written down:

J	A	M	E	S		N	A	S	H
1	1	4	5	1		5	1	1	8

The total of these numbers should then be added up: 1 add 1 add 4 add 5 add 1 add 5 add 1 add 1 add 8 is 27. The 2 and the 7 should then be added together because to get a lucky number it is necessary to go on adding any two numbers until a single number is achieved.

The lucky number for James Nash is therefore 9. Anyone with this lucky number should always choose it when buying raffle tickets, etc. Apart from that however, a look at numerologists' charts indicate the sort of personality a person represented by '9' should have. A 9 is represented by the figure of Prudence and therefore the person whose lucky number this is, is one who will make cautious judgements, is discreet, and whose rewards will result from deserving hard work.

All the children will obviously work out a lucky number for themselves, and have fun consulting their own numerological character study. Apart from 9 the others are as follows:

1   is represented by the figure of the Juggler. This person will be decisive in action, a natural leader and have a powerful personality.

2   is represented by the goddess Juno. This person will be home loving, not keen on competing with others, sensitive and always ready to be self-sacrificing.

3   the figure here is the Empress. This person is likely to be a good entertainer, good at making people laugh and keen on music.

4   is represented by the Key Bearer and this person is likely to be an extremely hard worker; very down-to-earth and a solid, reliable type.

5   is represented by the Magician and this person is likely to be restless; very competitive; sometimes rebellious and looking for changes.

6   is represented by Venus and symbolises a person who is happy, contented and will always try to seek peaceful solutions for other people.

7   is represented by Victory and this person is likely to be very successful, win many honours and become famous – but also be lonely as a result.

8   is represented by the figure of Justice and this person is likely to be determined and not afraid of trouble and argument in seeking what they think is right.

Once all this investigation and speculation has been done the children can compare themselves with people of similar 'lucky numbers' – do they have the same characteristics and strengths? Some interesting discussions could ensue!

Letters and words

Victorian Christmas activities often included large family gatherings playing various word games. In my experience children still enjoy these, and the two which follow are well suited to capable top juniors and older children.

Name that word

This activity calls for careful thinking and helps increase vocabulary. It can be played as follows:
1 From a pack of letters of the alphabet, one is drawn at random. Let us imagine it is M.
2 The children are then put into groups and told that each group will get a chance to choose an adjective beginning with M – to complete the following sentence:
'Father Christmas likes you because you are . . . .'
(merry, magnificent, marvellous, mischevious, magical, magnetic, modest, majestic, manly, massive, muscular, masterful, mathematical, mechanical, meek, mellow, melodic, memorable, merciful, meteoric, methodical, microscopic, mysterious, mighty, mobile, modern, monumental, monstrous, mountainous, musical)

It can be seen that this is not particularly easy and if it is played verbally a stop will soon be reached and a new letter required. This of course would be fine if only a short time is being allowed, but there is much to be said for allowing the groups to use dictionaries and make lists – the winners being the group with the longest correct list.

Alternatives are to modify the starting sentence, for example 'Father Christmas does *not* like you because you are . . . .' or rephrase it so that adverbs or nouns are required instead of adjectives.

Christmas Snakes and Ladders

Make copies of the snakes and ladders diagram below for the children to complete using the clues to find the words. For teacher convenience the solutions are completed in the diagram. (**A** stands for across and **D** for down.)

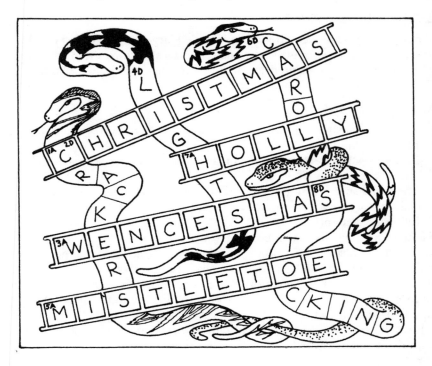

1A A favourite season of the year.
2D Pull and .... go bang.
3A A king remembered in a carol.
4D Seen at their best on a Christmas tree.
5A Something you might want to stand under.
6D A song used especially at this time of the year.
7A 'The ..... and the ivy.'
8D Usually contains a foot, but not always at Christmas.

Complete the story

In order to complete the following passage it is necessary to work out the missing words. Where a word is missing from the text, a clue is given which relates to how the word fits into the letter boxes.

One way of administering this game would be to dictate the passage – having first written the numbered boxes up on the blackboard for the children to copy. As the story progresses the children should try to fill in the boxes on their papers. (Solutions are written in for convenience here.)

Text to be read out:

1A of the most famous writers about Christmas was Charles Dickens. **2D 3D** a famous book called *A Christmas Carol*. **4A** of the great characters in this book was **5D** Scrooge. Scrooge was a very **6A** man who would not give anybody anything at Christmas. That is, **7D** he saw the ghosts. After **8D** he changed completely and became a much more generous **9D**.

Find the missing word

Write the crossword frame up on the board or provide copies of it. The clues can be written down or read out.

1A   Melchior, Balthazar and _____
2D   'O Come all ye _____'
2A   _____ Christmas
3D   Usually at Christmas we pull _____
3A   Marzipan is one ingredient in a Christmas _____
4A   The _____ scene has Joseph and Mary in it.
4D   'Follow the _____ to Bethlehem.'
5D   Invitations are usually needed to attend a _____

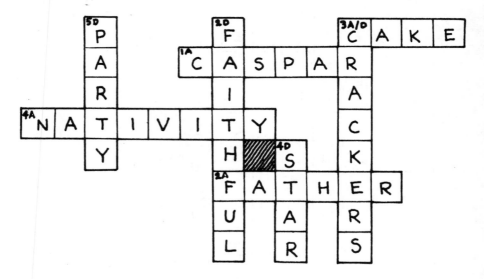

Figure 2

Play that word

This is another activity which can be done by either individuals or groups and again, with children, the latter seems preferable.

The arrangement is that one group decides on a word of two syllables and then in two separate mimes they give acting performances which provide clues to each of the syllables. The watchers must decide what the syllables are and then give the complete word in their answer. The group which first answers correctly gives the next performance – and so on.

Useful words might include:

Sunday	rainbow	eyebrow	eyelash	outlook
outpost	outside	swordfish	saltcellar	bullrush
roadworks	restful	pickpocket	peephole	passage
lighthouse	lifeless	hornpipe	hopeless	headlines
wheelbarrow	carport	forage	flagstaff	drumbeat
dashboard	carpet	castaway	breakfast	armour

Messages

Children enjoy activities with codes and the following can be related to Christmas. The first thing to comment on is the anagram. The children could be told that an anagram is a puzzle in which the letters of one (or more) words can be used to make another word. A few examples, with clues, might be put on the board to illustrate this. For example,

Word	*Clue*	*Anagram*
add	your father	dad
horse	by the seaside	shore
bugs die	in a cage	budgies
dew	to marry	wed
regal	very big	large
leap	without much colour	pale
pore	used for tying	rope
rate	shows when sad	tear
bleat	used with chairs	table
sail	is ill	ails

Having grasped the idea the children could be given the following passage to read. It contains six anagrams of words associated with Christmas. Teachers might feel that with some children it would be an advantage to underline the anagrams.

John was a keen horseman. When he shouted, 'Rest Mare,' to his horse she would stand quite still. He kept her feed in a cask, or bin, which stood at an angle to the stable door. He made sure the stable was always clear of rats. The final touch was the mare's name above the door. It was an unusual one and read, Ryam.

The anagrams in the passage are underlined; capital letters should be ignored in finding the solutions which are:

streamer sack robin angel star Mary

The second code activity is where selected words in a passage make up a hidden message. The code used in the passage below is an easy one to break but to write a message in it requires careful creation of sentences. Thus both 'breaking' and 'creating' are useful exercises.

The way to crack the code is to take the words immediately after place names and then arrange them to make a message.

> Father Christmas left Lapland at 8pm to travel to London. Midnight saw him at Dover. 'Go this way,' said an airborne sign. Underneath the sign it said, 'London, to the right.' In London, Julian's house was his first stop.
> *Coded message*: At midnight go to Julian's.

Where did you say?

The first requirement in this activity is for the teacher to get an atlas, select some well-known towns and cities, and then reproduce them in jumbled letter form on long, numbered strips of paper, one for every child. Some pins are also needed for this exercise.

Once the jumbled towns have been prepared, each of the children is given a piece of paper and directed to write 1 to 30 on it (or whatever number of children there are present).

The teacher then attaches a strip of paper to the back of each child with the pins. The children are then allowed to mingle and try and work out as many solutions as possible. The tricky one of course is that which is on their own back and which they cannot see. To solve this problem they must ask a friend to give them the letters on their own back – a stern test of friendship and co-operation when all are working at speed!

Draw it

To initiate this activity the teacher must first of all write down on separate pieces of paper the names of about twenty objects which are not easy to draw for identification purposes. For example, video, haystack, billiard cue, wallet, worm, field, blackberry, biscuit, blanket, chalk, chess board, corn, gas-fire, discus, rubber, fire extinguisher, hair dryer, jelly, typewriter, thimble. It must be remembered that there is very limited time for drawing/finding solutions.

The pieces of paper containing the words are then folded and put into a container. The class should be split into two groups. When this has been done, at a given signal, one person from each group comes out to the front.

The teacher then takes out a piece of paper and shows the word on it to the two children.

They then go back to their teams and attempt to draw the object (without saying anything of course). Once one team has got the right answer it scores a point. Two different members of the teams then go to receive a new clue. Naturally the winning team is the one which gets the most objects correct.

Can you read minds?

Children love tricks and the one described here has the great advantage of being easy to do. The instructions are written out so that they can be read directly to the children . . . .

Read this very carefully and you will learn how to play a very good trick on your friends. Don't try it on someone who has read it already!

All this trick needs is a pack of cards and a few people. Before doing anything else, you tell the people that you have made a fantastic discovery – you are capable of *ESP – EXTRA SENSORY PERCEP-TION*. In other words you can tell what somebody is thinking by just laying your hands on their heads!

Having told your audience this they will, of course, not believe you, so you have to prove it.

Take the pack of cards and ask one of the group to pick a card. Ask this person to look at and to remember which card it is, and then give it back to you without letting you see what it is.

Take this card in your hand with the back facing you. Put the rest of the cards on the floor.

Next, hold the card in your right hand and face it to the audience. Say the following to them:

'I don't know what this card is but I am showing it to all of you. In a moment I am going to rest my hands on your heads and the messages I receive will tell me what this card is. Please take careful note of it.'

Whilst you are saying this, very earnestly and seriously, to the audience, you should be squeezing the card in and out in your right hand – as if to draw attention to it. A quick glance at the card whilst you are doing this will show you what it is when it is bent.

Remember you must do this very cleverly so that nobody suspects what you are doing. Make sure the audience are concentrating on what you are saying when you take your glance.

The next step is to ask somebody to come from the group and take the card from your hand – without letting you see it. Then ask

Figure 3

someone else to pick up the pack of cards – and a third person to put in the chosen card and give the pack a shuffle.

When all this has been done you start your 'patter' again. Choose one or two people from the group, put your hands on their heads and see if you can 'read their minds' in order that they will 'tell' you what the chosen card is. As you already know what the card is you can choose your time and decide on the person whose 'message' gives you the 'answer'.

CHAPTER 11 🎄

Christmas contacts

Would you like to see nativity scenes made from everything from straw to glass – and originating from over thirty countries? Would you like more visual information about old Christmas 'frost fairs?' Would you like to take your children to a practical session entitled 'Make your own Christmas cards?'

Every year, in various parts of the country, exciting 'visit' possibilities such as these occur. This chapter seeks to provide information about useful contacts for possible Christmas activities, with some details of what these sources have provided in previous years. Such information is also very useful to children who may wish to follow up these activities with their parents during the holidays. In some instances the activities take place only during the Christmas holiday period.

Christmas contacts

London
Barbican Centre
Silk Street, London EC2 (01 638 4141)
Between 5 December 1984, and 8 January 1985, an exhibition was staged on the concourse of the Barbican, its theme was the art of the crib. Countries as far apart as Poland and Peru were represented, with nativity scenes made in a vast range of styles and materials.

The instigators of this exhibition were a firm called:
Christmas Archives
64 Severn Road, Cardiff CF1 9EA (0222 41120)
who also produce useful Christmas fact sheets for schools, for example, 'History of Christmas Customs/Cards/Decorations.'

Also on display at the Barbican (1984/85) was a 'Design a Christmas Card' exhibition made up of paintings and drawings by children aged between four and fifteen, and sponsored by Martins and 'Woman' magazine. Another spectacular exhibition was that of the designs created by E.J. Taylor for Tiffany's store windows in New York. These were based on the theme of St Nicholas.

Bethnal Green Museum of Childhood
Cambridge Heath Road, London E2 (01 980 2415)
This is an absolutely marvellous museum and a visit there with children is an enjoyable experience at any time of the year. At Christmas however this is especially so and requests as to what the current year's 'special' is, should be given high priority.

In recent years at Bethnal Green there have been workshops on Snow and Ice linked to the 'Spirit of Christmas' exhibition; stories, ballads and things to make in connection with the story of St Nicholas; a look at the 'three Kings' with references to art through the ages; eating at Christmas; music at Christmas; winter weather – including those 'frost fairs', and a magic lantern show.

Everything is always done with excellent taste and visits here are most rewarding.

Commonwealth Institute
Kensington High Street, London W8 (01 603 4535)
This has had some interesting story-telling sessions with Christmas stories from round the world. A special feature of Christmas, 1984, was an invitation to join in the traditional songs, dances and games, as well as stories, which form an essential part of Malta's Christmas celebrations.

Geffrye Museum
Kingsland Road, London E2 (01 739 8368)
This is another museum whose staff really understand the needs of children and teachers, and whose Christmas activities are always interesting. Recent years' activities have included talks on wartime Christmas; a Victoria Christmas; a Stuart Christmas; Christmas customs. There have also been Christmas workshops, puppet shows and the distribution of Christmas puzzle sheets.

Horniman Museum
London Road, Forest Hill, London SE23 (01 699 1872)
This museum has workshops and there was a recent one (1984) connected with a Norwegian Christmas. There have also been 'recreations' of an Elizabethan Christmas with music (using viols, lutes, crumhorns, etc.) and dancing.

Museum of London
London Wall, London EC2 (01 600 3699)
This museum has had a slide/tape presentation of the four seasons in London, and also workshops.

National Portrait Gallery
St Martin's Place, London WC2 (01 930 1552)
The gallery has had a workshop/project on entertaining a king (Henry VII).

National Gallery
Trafalgar Square, London WC2 (01 839 3321)
It often has Christmas quizzes with information sheets.

National Maritime Museum
Romney Road, London SE10 (01 858 4422)
Worth looking out for here are the planetarium shows in the Old Royal Observatory Buildings, one of which was the 'Star of Bethlehem.'

Tate Gallery
Millbank, London SW1 (01 821 7128)
In recent years this gallery has had a Christmas trail entitled 'Looking into Colour' which was suitable for top junior/lower secondary children. There have also been 'Spot the Detail' activities and, on a lighter note, the annual Christmas tree guessing game. In the latter, children are asked to guess how many cards are on a tree.

Theatres
A look at what is on offer at some of the little-known theatres is often as rewarding as checking on bigger productions.

Little Angel Marionette Theatre
14 Dagmar Passage, Cross Street, London N1 (01 226 1787)
This theatre has put on 'The Prince and the Mouse' and 'Amahl and the Night Visitors' in recent years.

Polka Children's Theatre
240 The Broadway, Wimbledon SW19 (01 543 4888)
This theatre has had puppet workshops as well as shows.

Royal Festival Hall
South Bank, London SE1 (01 928 3191)
This usually houses a feast of good things at Christmas. In the past these have included those very skilful musicians, the Musketts (Michael and Doreen), playing festive music on an enormous variety of instruments from medieval to modern; Christmas shows containing 'Hansel and Gretel' and traditional mummers' plays; music by Atarah and her band.

Birmingham and surrounding area
Birmingham Museum and Art Gallery
Chamberlain Square, Birmingham (021 235 2834)
They have had sessions on 'Make your own Christmas cards'; various gallery trails; 'Christmas food and feasting' with slides and recipes.

Midland Arts Centre, Cannon Hill Park, Birmingham (021 440 3838)
This has various workshops at set times during the Christmas holidays.

Blakesley Hall
Blakesley Road, Yardley.
The Hall has had sessions on Victorian Christmas presents, with advice on how children might attempt to make some of these.

Manchester
Athenaeum Art Gallery
81 Princess Street, Manchester (061 236 9283)
This gallery has had painting explorations and workshops during the holidays.

Manchester Museum
Oxford Road, Manchester (061 273 3333)
This museum has had a theme of 'In the Bleak Mid-Winter' which encouraged creative work.

Chester
Grosvenor Museum
27 Grosvenor Street, Chester (0224 21616)
This has held workshops including the making of Christmas cards, decorations, presents and food linked to Victorian Christmases.

Newcastle-upon-Tyne
Joicey Museum, City Road, Newcastle (0632 324 562)
The museum has had displays of period toys and costume, and the history of pantomime.

Sheffield
Mappin Art Gallery
Weston Park, Sheffield (0742 734 789)
This had a project which involved the Christmas story being portrayed in a range of materials.

Oxford and nearby
Museum of Oxford
St Aldates (0865 815 559)
The museum has arranged 'Design your own Victorian Christmas card' sessions.

Banbury Museum
8 Horsefair, Banbury (0295 598 555)
This has had sessions on making your own Victorian decorations.

Norwich and the surrounding area
Castle Museum, Norwich (0603 22233)
It has had exhibitions of 'Christmas Crafts at the Castle' when potters, engravers, toy makers, etc., have given demonstrations of their skills.

Elizabethan House Museum
4 South Quay, Great Yarmouth (0493 55746)
This museum has had an exhibition which welcomed school parties and provided a magic lantern show, a display of Victorian and Edwardian toys, games and mechanical music, and talks about Christmas customs in the past.

CHAPTER 12

Different Christmases

The purpose of this chapter was to offer some comments on Christmases very different to those enjoyed by most people in Great Britain today. The aim was to find differences in both time and place.

Two of the Christmases described here are taped interviews with people of very different backgrounds. Sue Payne spoke of her Christmases now in Sydney, Australia: Kvetinka Lunts spoke of the memories of Christmas in Czechoslovakia in the 1930s. The third 'reflection' is again very different and was the result of a talk with a service manager in a leading Berlin car agency about a very special Christmas.

A modern Christmas in Australia

Sue Payne is a young lady who lives in Sydney, Australia. Before going to Australia she lived in England. She is married to the owner of a health food shop and she herself is an aerobics dancing teacher. Both she and her husband enjoy the outdoor life. The following is a transcript of an interview with her.

Author 'I'd like to ask you about some of the ways in which Christmas in Australia differs from Christmas in Britain.'

Sue 'Well for a start, when you wake up the sky is likely to be very blue, the sun yellow and the temperature very high.'

Author 'What time does it actually start to get light in the morning?'

Sue 'At this time of the year it is light by 5am.'

Author 'Has the whole place got a Christmas atmosphere? Is it full of decorations for instance? Are there trees about and carol singers?'

Sue 'No – it is not at all like the "Christmas atmosphere" in Britain. You do hear carols, people do have Christmas trees, and they can also be seen in shops, but if you are used to a European Christmas it is very strange to see everybody walking round in shorts and T-shirts.'

Author 'Do most people have Christmas dinner as we know it here?'

Sue 'Yes.'

Author 'Do they have it at midday or in the evening?'

Sue 'Australians have festive food like turkey and ham but it is often eaten outside at a barbecue.'

Author 'When do people exchange presents?'

Sue 'This depends a great deal on people's upbringing. Many go to midnight mass on Christmas Eve and exchange and open presents on their return; others open them when they get up on Christmas morning. It is really an individual choice.'

Author 'Is there a feeling of Christmas being a great religious festival in Sydney?'

Sue 'Oh yes. Services in all churches are very well attended. I attended a Catholic mass at midnight last Christmas and it was a very beautiful service.'

Author 'Are the services mostly at midnight?'

Sue 'Yes.'

Author 'Are there many people from other parts of the world celebrating Christmas in Sydney?'

Sue 'There seems to be an enormous number of different ethnic groups celebrating "their" Christmases at this time of the year. There are Greeks, Italians, Poles – groups from almost every European country.'

Author 'Do these groups celebrate Christmas in their own churches? Are they in separate sections of Sydney?'

Sue 'The answer to both of these questions is yes. For instance, most Greek people tend to be in one particular part of the city, and so do the other nationalities. This tends to give a particular European or Asian flavour to some parts of the city.'

Author 'Do the shops start their Christmas advertising and displays as early as they do in Britain?'

Sue 'No.'

Author 'When do the first things start appearing?'

Sue 'Middle to late November.'

Author 'Do the Christmas displays try and portray the season as one of snow and ice?'

Sue 'Yes, despite the fact that the temperature may be about 100°F there is still the attempt to portray a "White Christmas."'

Author Do children go out and sing carols in the streets?'

Sue	'No.'
Author	'Does anybody go out carol singing?'
Sue	'You don't get the door to door carol singing like you do in Britain but there is a great deal of carol singing in public parks and on the beaches as well as in the churches.'
Author	'Are there any focal points such as huge Christmas trees?'
Sue	'Yes, there is a very big Christmas tree in Martin Place which is one of the landmarks of Sydney and this is the equivalent to the one in Trafalgar Square in London.'
Author	'How do you personally feel about British and Australian
Sue	Christmases?'
	'When I think of a British Christmas I think of going to church muffled in warm clothes and then coming back to spend the day with the family, being cosy, eating traditional food, playing games, watching TV together. When I think of an Australian Christmas I think of being outside, enjoying the company of family and friends on the beach, and doing absolutely everything out of doors.'
Author	'Do you prefer one to the other?'
Sue	'No, Christmas seems equally special in both places.'

Christmas in Czechoslovakia before the Second World War

Before the Second World War began Kvetinka Lunts was a child growing up in a tiny village in Czechoslovakia. She had a Czech father and an English mother. Before the Germans took over the area where she lived her family fled to Britain where her father was interned as an alien. Kwet (Kvetinka) has now got a Polish husband and a grown-up family of her own – but she spoke with great nostalgia for the distant Christmases of her childhood.

Author	'Where did you spend your early childhood in the 1930s?'
Kwet	'In a little village called Mistrovice in the South Carpathian mountains, almost on the border of Russia; tucked away between Russia and Austria really, and not near any big town.'
Author	'But it was actually part of Czechoslovakia at that time?'
Kwet	'Oh yes, it was – and we felt very strongly about that, although the Sudeten German land came pretty near.'
Author	'What language did you speak there?'
Kwet	'The people spoke German and Czech. Everybody could speak both but the German was a sort of slang version. However I had an English mother and I grew up speaking English, German and Czech and this made things difficult for me.'

Author	'In what sort of circumstances did you live in this village?'
Kwet	'My grandfather was the local doctor and we lived in a big house so I didn't really mix much with the village children at all except for parties and things like that.'
Author	'Would you say that Christmas in Czechoslovakia at that time was very different from Christmas in Britain now?'
Kwet	'Oh yes, very different indeed.'
Author	'Were there religious differences?'
Kwet	'Yes – well, I don't think Christmas over here is very religious for many people is it? In those days in Mistrovice you always had a fast on Christmas Eve and up to then it was much more of build-up – rather like you have here during Lent. After the fast we went to church and that sort of ended the build-up to Christmas. Now it was actually here!'
Author	'What about "traditional" food?'
Kwet	'It was very different. We had fish – always one very big dish of fish which was always dressed up to look very beautifully decorative. Then we used to have pork mostly after that. There also used to be a gorgeous smell of cinnamon biscuits – everything seemed to smell of cinnamon. We made cinnamon biscuits to give to all callers at the house, and then we decorated the tree with them. We children used to put ribbons through the biscuits – big ones, small ones – and hang them up. These biscuits were one of the main decorations on the tree.'
Author	'That's interesting – there doesn't seem to be anything like that here does there?'
Kwet	'Oh yes – I still do it at home now! We did have glass decorations in Mistrovice but they were very very precious. They came out every year for use and the thought of breaking one was just too terrible to even consider. It was a tragedy if a tail fell off a peacock!'
Author	'Have you got an outstanding memory of Christmas time in those days?'
Kwet	'Yes – of St Nicholas coming round with his servant Black Peter.'
Author	'On December 6 you mean?'
Kwet	'Knocking on the door . . . . and you held your breath because he asked, "Has anybody been naughty?" And if you had been you were promised a wallop instead of a present. Oh yes, I can still remember that, holding my breath with dread of Black Peter, especially if I'd fallen foul with somebody the day before.'
Author	'What about children there and then? Did they behave any differently from children today?'

Kwet	'Children? In general?'
Author	'Yes, do you think they appreciated small presents more then? Were they more captivated by the atmosphere?'
Kwet	'Oh yes, we were captivated by the whole atmosphere, but I'm not sure that children aren't even now. There is just much more of everything now, and it's much earlier . . . . although our Christmases went on much longer because Epiphany was very important.'
Author	'How was that?'
Kwet	'We didn't feel the season was over until Epiphany. The "three kings" came to everybody's house with the priest. They blessed the house and were asked in and given iced cakes and drinks. Then when they left they would write over the door post the initials of the three kings - M, B, C, and the date, and that stayed there until the next Christmas.'
Author	'I don't think we had such "romantic" Christmases as continental people.'
Kwet	'Well, I think you were further advanced over here at that time. Perhaps village life was ending here, but over there then it was still a very small isolated community. I also think, in a way, "religion" in Britain is taken more seriously.'
Author	'How do you mean?'
Kwet	'Well, in Mistrovice it was just part of our ordinary life and I don't know that we thought about it very deeply. It was just an integral part of life.'
Author	'Was there a pattern to Christmas day itself?'
Kwet	'No – I can't recall anything particularly extraordinary. I mostly remember going down for the presents because we had them downstairs – they were left on the window-sill.'
Author	'And when did you exchange your presents?'
Kwet	'In the morning just like we do now – but of course that may have been because I had an English mother!'
Author	'Can you tell me any more about church services in Mistrovice at Christmas?'
Kwet	'Yes, I was the youngest of seven children, and the oldest of these went with my parents to midnight mass. Then the whole family went again to a family service on Christmas day.'
Author	'When did you get the feeling that Christmas was really starting? Here it seems to get so much earlier each year.'
Kwet	'Well, really my first impressions of Christmas approaching were through the cooking. The whole house was full of lovely smells as the cooking for Christmas started – and I suppose this was at the

Author   beginning of December. Back to that smell of cinnamon again! We also used to make lots of little gifts for each other and we started sewing things before Christmas. That was all part of it.'

Author   'What about carol singing. Did people do that?'

Kwet   'Yes, but only the day before Christmas, and the carol singers were the choristers from church. They would come in a group and sing, and then be invited into the house. It was lovely.'

Author   'Was the weather significantly different in that part of the world?'

Kwet   'Well I remember there being snow every year at Christmas, but perhaps this is just a child's memory!'

Christmas 1947, remembered by a former German prisoner-of-war in Britain

By Christmas, 1947 the Second World War had been over for more than a year. There was still however many German prisoners-of-war left in Britain. Imprisoned in camps throughout the country they often worked as farm labourers during the day, returning to their prison camps at night. It was decided that if local people were prepared to take these prisoners into their homes on Christmas day, they would be given special 24-hour passes to leave their camps. Freddy, went with two other POWs to a house in a small Yorkshire village . . . .

'We had been in camps for so long the first wonderful thing was to be inside a proper home again. Of course we did not know how the people would feel about us. Not so long ago we had been the enemy.

When we got to the door of the house and knocked a lady asked us to come in. None of us could speak English well. We stood there feeling awkward and embarrassed and then the man of the house shook hands with us, looking very stern as he did so. I thought it was going to be awful, I think we all did, until suddenly the door leading to the stairs burst open and two children rushed in.

One was a little girl who reminded me of my own child back in Berlin. She headed straight for me, and with a giggle began pulling at my trouser legs. I bent down and lifted her up high above my head. She let out a great cry of laughter, and suddenly, everybody was laughing! It no longer seemed to matter that we did not speak each other's language.

Soon we were all sitting round a large old-fashioned table "talking" in bits of German and bits of English and some sign language. I can remember as clearly as if it were yesterday what we had to eat. There was beef, and although there wasn't much of it for any of us, it was well cooked and served with lots of lentils. I could tell that the pudding was made with dried egg rather than the real thing, and there weren't many currants in it. On each plate a little piece of holly was laid beside the pudding.

It doesn't sound very much now but at the time it seemed a marvellous meal. We knew that everything was rationed and that by having us in their home this family had to go without themselves.

After we had eaten, a bottle of port was brought out of a deep, dark cupboard. The adults solemnly toasted each other whilst the children disappeared, returning quickly with small parcels and big, home-made Christmas cards. A bit shy now, they handed my two friends and myself a parcel each. Soon I was looking down at an unwrapped cigar.

Then it was our turn to surprise our hosts. Once we had heard the wonderful news that we were to be allowed to spend Christmas in a family home, each man had used his imagination! So now we handed over our presents – slippers, made with cloth and stuffed with straw, and tiny carvings which we had worked on.

After the exchange of presents the fire was poked and the small room warmed with the people in it. We prisoners lit our precious cigars and suddenly, unexpectedly, we were singing carols – German and English, one after the other. It was hard to keep back the tears as my friends and I sang 'Stille Nacht' and thought about our own families whom we had not seen for such a long time.

And then, an unforgettable Christmas was over. As we marched back to camp we were silent, each thinking his own thoughts of Christmases past, and wondering what madness had overtaken the world in these last few years.'

Postscript

Most of this book has been concerned with practical considerations which involve teachers and children at Christmas. It may therefore, in conclusion, be useful to step outside of this basically practical approach and consider the views of an eminent theologian when he poses that question which children still ask, and usually in exactly the same words:

What really happened?

'I was saying yesterday that if we don't allow for the fact that the gospels were written after Jesus' resurrection, and in the light of all that his disciples experienced the risen Jesus to be, then the stories they tell of his birth and infancy sounded like fairy tales. It's because I know that a lot of people do regard them as fairy tales, and dismiss them as unworthy of their consideration, that I am anxious to say more on this subject. I want to try and show something of the depth contained in these apparently naive stories.

You see, supposing you and I had been present at Jesus' birth and someone asked us, 'What really happened?', we might have replied, 'Well, nothing out of the ordinary. A Jewish builder, his wife, poor people, a baby was born.'

Now the gospel writer would say to that, 'What a shallow way of looking at it! Why don't you look deeper? In the light of all that this child eventually proved to be, in view of all that came out of this event, are you just going to say 'a baby was born'. How about a bit of excitement? What really happened? What *really* happened was that the Son of God was born, and the whole of the heavens rejoiced. This was *the* decisive moment in history. God was in this apparently trivial event. I can't use humdrum language to say that.'

But now do you see what happens? If you and I are naive in the way we read his account, and don't appreciate the poetry, we've returned to the shallow level we started with. We'll say, 'Your account is all about angels and stars and voices. It's all about the kind of things which never happen in the sort of world I live in. What really happened? Obviously something which is nothing like the sort of things that happen to me.'

But the truth is that what happened is exactly like what happens to you and me, in exactly the sort of world we live in, if only you and I had eyes to see it.

This is terribly important to understand, otherwise we gradually lose touch with God altogether. God no one has ever seen. But if he really is in contact with us, if he really does enter into a relationship with us, we've got to speak in concrete images and express ourselves in visual terms. And that's what the Bible does. What else can a poet do? But if we take those images literally, as if God's activity was visible, then the Bible becomes a never-never land . . . .

. . . We live in a world where God is hidden, and we can't see him. We can only know of his presence in faith. It's a world where nothing interrupts the order of nature. Our lives are very ordinary lives. What use could we have for a religion which is out of this world? We need something which tells us what our ordinary lives are about. We can't be helped by hearing about people who saw what we can't see.

I really believe that the Bible isn't trying to tell us about another fancy world. I believe that it really does, in its picturesque way, tell us about ordinary people like you and me, living through the ordinary events that you and I know, only they saw them in depth, with the eyes of faith.

The Bible tells us above all about Jesus, and it tells us that he is like you and me. It's by looking at Jesus that I really see what I can be. Jesus is the truth about us. If he were not, if he were only some visitor from outer space, how could what is written about him be good news for us?

from *The First Christmas – What Really Happened?*, H. J. Richards